ARTS IN SOCIETY

**Published by Research and
Statewide Programs in the Arts
University of Wisconsin–Extension**

EDITOR
Edward Kamarck

ASSOCIATE EDITOR
Monika Jensen

ASSISTANT EDITOR
D. Jean Collins

ART EDITOR
Linda Heddle

POETRY EDITOR
Felix Pollak

ADMINISTRATIVE SECRETARY
Lorraine Graves

EDITORIAL SECRETARY
Mary McCoy

CIRCULATION MANAGER
Linda Heddle

ADVERTISING MANAGER
Jane Schwichtenberg

PUBLICATION CONSULTANT
Donald Kaiser

PRODUCTION CONSULTANT
John Gruber

This issue was designed by Linda Heddle
with the assistance of Linda Rich.

Arts in Society is dedicated to the augment-
ing of the arts in society and to the
advancement of education in the arts. These
publications are to be of interest, therefore, both to the professional and the lay
public. Arts in Society exists to discuss,
interpret, and illustrate the various functions
of the arts in contemporary civilization. Its
purpose is to present the insights of
experience, research and theory in support
of educational and organizational efforts to
enhance the position of the arts in America.
In general, four areas are dealt with: the
teaching and learning of the arts; aesthetics
and philosophy; social analysis; and significant examples of creative expression in a
medium which may be served by the
printing process.

The editors will welcome articles on any
subjects which fall within the areas of interest of this journal. Readers both in the
United States and abroad are invited to submit manuscripts for consideration for publication. Articles may be written in the
contributor's native language. An
honorarium will be paid for papers accepted
for publication.

Manuscripts should be sent to: Edward
Kamarck, Editor, Arts in Society, University
of Wisconsin–Extension, 610 Langdon Street,
Madison, Wisconsin 53706. Address review
copies of books, recordings, tapes and films
to the same address.

We regret that due to our large stock of
poetry and limited staff time, we are not
reviewing or soliciting poetry.

Advertising rates available upon request.
For **subscription information,** see page 173.

Copyright, 1974, by the Regents of the
University of Wisconsin System.

TABLE OF CONTENTS

Women and the Arts

Volume 11, Number 1   Spring-Summer 1974

BOARD OF CONTRIBUTING AND ADVISORY EDITORS

Vivienne Anderson
Director, Division of the Humanities and the Arts, State Education Department, University of the State of New York.

Tracy Atkinson
Director, Milwaukee Art Center.

Tino Balio
Director, Wisconsin Center for Theatre Research, the University of Wisconsin–Madison.

Albert Bermel
Playwright and translator, teaches theatre history and criticism at Columbia and Julliard.

Herbert Blau
Theatre director and educator, Oberlin College.

Warren Bower
Literary critic and professor of English at New York University.

Gilbert Chase
Writer and lecturer on the arts and the history of ideas.

Donald Clark
Dean, College of Fine Arts, The University of Oklahoma.

Robert Corrigan
Arts educator, critic, and writer on the arts.

Junius Eddy
Arts consultant, Arts in Education Program, the Rockefeller Foundation.

Hy Faine
Director, Management in the Arts Program, University of California, Los Angeles.

Morgan Gibson
Poet and educator, Goddard College.

Freda Goldman
Director, Continuing Education for Women, University Extension, The University of Rhode Island.

Stella Gray
Chairman, Division of Humanistic Studies, University of Wisconsin–Parkside.

William Hanford
Dean, School of the Arts, University of Wisconsin–Stevens Point.

Ihab Hassan
Vilas Research Professor of English and Comparative Literature at the University of Wisconsin–Milwaukee.

Frederick Haug
Dean, College of Arts and Sciences, University of Wisconsin–Eau Claire.

John B. Hightower
President, Associated Councils of the Arts.

Richard Hunt
Sculptor, Chicago.

Bernard James
Professor of Anthropology at the University of Wisconsin–Milwaukee and Director of the Center for Advanced Study in Organizational Science in University Extension.

Abbott Kaplan
President, College at Purchase, State University of New York.

Max Kaplan
Director, Institute for Studies of Leisure, The University of South Florida.

Eugene Kaelin
Aesthetician, writer on the arts, and Professor of Philosophy at Florida State University.

Irving Kaufman
Professor, Department of Art, The City College of the City University of New York.

Frances Kinne
Dean, College of Fine Arts, Jacksonville University.

Richard Kostelanetz
Writer and lecturer on the arts.

Irving Kreutz
Chairman, Department of English, University of Wisconsin–Extension.

Raymond Light
Dean, College of the Arts, University of Wisconsin–Whitewater.

Frederick Logan
Professor of Art and Art Education, University of Wisconsin–Madison.

Jack Morrison
Associate Director, Arts in Education, John D. Rockefeller III Fund.

Linda Nochlin
Writer and Professor of Art History, Vassar College.

Norman Rice
Dean, The School of Fine Arts, Carnegie-Mellon University.

Edouard Roditi
Poet and critic.

James Rosenberg
Professor of Drama at Carnegie-Mellon University.

Allen Sapp
Executive Director, American Council for the Arts in Education.

Alan Schneider
Theatre director, critic and educator.

Barry Schwartz
Author, poet, lecturer on Humanism and Culture, and Director of the Cultural Alternatives Network.

Marcia Siegel
Dance critic of the *Hudson Review*.

Adolph Suppan
Dean, School of Fine Arts, University of Wisconsin–Milwaukee.

Fannie Taylor
Director, Office of Program Information, National Endowment for the Arts.

Harold Taylor
Educator, philosopher, lecturer on the arts.

Walter H. Walters
Dean, College of Arts and Architecture, Pennsylvania State University.

Allen S. Weller
Dean, College of Fine and Applied Arts, University of Illinois.

Peter Yates
Chairman, Music Department, State University College at Buffalo.

A SHIFT IN THE BALANCE

Women and the Arts Conference, Wingspread. Photo by Bob Black. Courtesy: The Johnson Foundation.

All human relations have shifted—those between masters and servants, husbands and wives, parents and children. And when human relations change there is at the same time a change in religion, conduct, politics and literature.

—Virginia Woolf

Today, even more than in Virginia Woolf's day human relations have shifted and are in the process of shifting still more. Nowhere is such shifting more apparent than in those areas of life which are affected by the growing consciousness and activism of women. Ms. Woolf appropriately places her final emphasis on literature and art for it is here where we search for and hope to find the honest reflections of our psychological and social reality and the inspiration to change that reality, when necessary, to create a more human society.

This special issue devoted to *Women and the Arts* represents both a physical and a spiritual coming together of women (and some men) to look at women in the arts within the context of the social issues of today and as an outgrowth and integral part of the movement by many groups to create a more human environment for all.

The core of the issue grew out of the thinking, discussion and writing of the one hundred artists, writers, homemakers, volunteers, administrators, critics, and educators who attended a conference on Women and the Arts at Wingspread, the Johnson Foundation Conference Center near Racine, Wisconsin on September 13-15, 1973.* The works in this collection reflect the major emphases of the conference: that historical and contemporary images of women are transmitted through the arts and that they influence societal expectations and values, including those that women have of themselves; that women's inner images determine their relationship with the world at large; that this relationship must include active participation by women in shaping society; that social reform is a prerequisite to the creation of new cultural values and conversely that new "humanist-feminist" values must direct such reform; and that one area of necessary change is cultural institutions which must be made more responsive to the needs of all of society's members. Those pieces in the issue including the poetry and book reviews which did not grow out of the conference directly are nevertheless tangential to these concerns.

The women who speak in this issue reflect multifarious viewpoints and modes of expression. But the underlying theme for all of their expression is similar—art is socially important and the creative process of art is essential to the union of self and image, society and art, institutional resource and individual need.

The articles, reviews, poetry, discussion and pictures in this issue present only a glimpse of the network of supportive women in the arts in all parts of the country who shared their energy, enthusiasm and superb intelligence with us. We are deeply grateful to everyone who helped with the planning and execution of the conference and issue. We give special thanks to Kathryn Clarenbach, to Rita Goodman of The Johnson Foundation and to the members of the Conference Planning Committee** for their invaluable advice and assistance in bringing this project to fruition.

L.M.H.
M.R.J.

*Other developments of the conference are state and national organizations of Women in the Arts. Please contact our editorial offices for further information. (See page 173.)
**The members of the Conference Planning Committee are listed with all of the conference participants on page 168 of this issue.

Macarena Esperanza by Audrey Flac

by Elizabeth Janeway
Author and critic.

When I began to think about the subject of the Conference on Women and the Arts, I discovered that I was involved in a running dispute with myself even before I began to write. Before I could begin to discuss the image of woman and its relationship to art, I had to clarify a confusion in my head about another relationship. I think it is one that is germane to our topic, however, and especially to any action that we may aspire to take in remaking the image of woman traditional in our society. So let me begin by stating the question that has been nagging at me: How does "image" relate to "self"? Are they the same thing? Is the image *a* way, or *the* way, in which we project the self? Or is it, perhaps, a way in which we know the self? And, if we are indeed facing the task of changing the image of woman to something more positive than it has been in the past, what will the shifting of one side of the relationship mean for the other?

Is the image the self? The idea is repugnant. Are we only what we seem to be? Surely the suggestion that we are just that is the source of a great deal of the anger and frustration that women have felt for so long and have only recently been able to bring up to consciousness and confront openly. All of us, I imagine, would deny that our true, felt, identity can be defined by an image stamped on us like a seal drawn by the outside world. We have felt for a long time that the assigned image of woman, acted out in the role-behavior expected of us, has not offered us self-fulfillment but, rather, has functioned as mask, as screen, as armor— most of all, as barrier between the inner self and the world. Whatever the momentary pattern of that image, every woman who has ever lived would surely cry out, "It is not I."

But in a curious way this alienation between the self and the image, necessary though it may be for the very survival of the self, has contributed to the continuing life of the image. We are, as Simone de Beauvoir saw and said so well, not only the second sex, but the *other* sex. Our alienation has sustained this otherness. Perceptive men have spoken for centuries of the mysterious woman, the female enigma, hiding her inner qualities from the world. Upon this blank space, this turned-away face of the self, they have projected their desires and fancies, time out of mind. Fertility fetish from the caves of the Stone Age, virgin goddess, all-giving mother, demoniac maenad, sybilline prophetess, malign witch, angel in the house, golden-hearted whore, we have been all these things and more. When Virginia Woolf's father was courting her mother he wrote her, "You must let me tell you that I do and always shall feel for you something which I can only call reverence as well as love. You see, I have not got any saints and you must not be angry if I put you in the place where my saints ought to be." Perhaps Julia Duckworth, whose warm, loving portrait her daughter drew in *To the Lighthouse* as Mrs. Ramsay, knitting away on a sock for one of the children, might have preferred to be a plain human being, but Leslie Stephen decreed otherwise. Sainthood was thrust upon her, and we can only admire her ability to carry off the role.

And indeed many women have carried off unexpected and probably less welcome roles while they hid their own inner qualities from the world. Often, I think, they must have hugged to themselves, as their greatest treasure, the unknown self within the image, the sensitive feeling mind. On occasion that mind has surely seen the world more clearly and realistically than a man can do, for often *his* mind is entangled with the sentiment and principle that appear to be needed by those charged with sustaining and justifying the structure of an imperfect world; the sentiments and

9

principles and prejudices embodied in the mythology of any society. Imprisoned in her image, the feminine mind has sometimes questioned that mythology, turning on it a gaze so cold, so cynical if you will, that men who have felt its penetration have drawn back in terror. For this is a view removed from the possibility of action, and therefore from the need to justify that action by setting up pious reasons for its validity. It is the view of she who is not doer, but done-to; and done-to, acted-upon, manipulated by the pious reasons of others, what revenge can the passive observer hope for except to see clearly, with mordant, unwavering gaze, the way it is, the course that action takes? If we can do nothing but *see,* then our unused energies will force us to see to the bottom, to the last grain of vanity and self-deceit and vain aspiration in those who act. We will follow sardonically the course of action, unmoved ourselves by failure or success since we have had no hand in achieving either one and know only that all action ends at last in the grave. Women have been blamed for that view often enough, told they are disloyal and, of course, "deadlier than the male." So we can be satisfied that it is part of our image too.

I believe it is a very important part of the image because it is an expression of the irreducible self and I believe further that our first task in remaking or re-creating the image of woman is to call on the energy and the reality of the self within the image. So I ask you, for a moment, to consider with me that silent observer within her interior tower. Even to other women she is hesitant to make herself known save by an occasional complicitous glance but she is there within us, casting her cold eye at the horsemen of the passing scene, whether we admit her presence or not. She is what bears and endures and survives, knowing and accepting with mocking amusement her distance and difference from the exterior image, whatever it may be: dutiful daughter, loving wife, nurturing mother. She is the thing that the image has bound but not murdered. I wish I knew what to call her. Yeats called her "Crazy Jane," and perhaps that will do for now since his poems incorporate both the loneliness of her existence and the sense that it is the world which is insane, not Jane

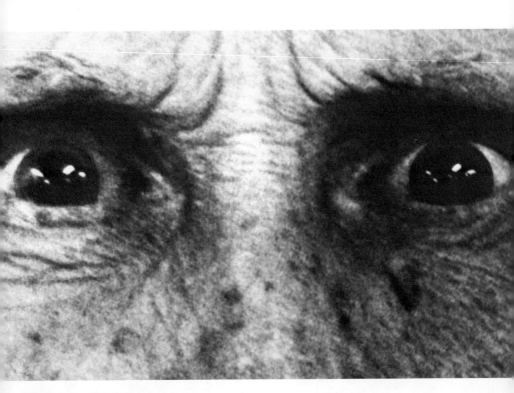

Photo by Sharon Ellis (University of Texas).

herself. But in the end, it is women who will have to name her, if we want to acknowledge her right not only to judge the world, but also to act upon it.

For this Jane of ours cannot stand apart in total isolation from her image, self-enclosed and self-sufficient. She cannot retreat into craziness and still be human. Repugnant as it may be to see ourselves in the image assigned to us by others, we cannot deny that vision entirely. No one can live alone. We human beings are social creatures in a very special sense, not simply because we depend on others for protection, like herd animals, but because we need other eyes and other minds to know our world, and ourselves. How can we understand the world at all and learn its working connections and processes, how can we ascribe significance to events, except through the teaching of those who were here when we were born? For we are born not just into a natural world as the animals are, but into the whole enormous expanse of a cultural heritage, a heritage that has to be learned, by every child, from the pre-existent system of imagery that our ancestors began to make when the first hand shaped the first tool.

It is the transmission of this heritage, of all the artifacts of the mind, of mythologies and conceptual structures, of science and technology, of ways of seeing and knowing from Kant to Castaneda, which makes us human and distinguishes man from beast. Indeed without our culture we are not even animals but mere naked abortions, for we have lost the inborn instincts which are given to animals for their journey through life. We have replaced these pre-programmed instructions in the genes with something quite else and quite different— with an ability to learn and also to *teach,* which means the ability to change both our world and ourselves. This capacity to learn, and then to pass on what we have learned by means of language, is uniquely human. It is the reason why we are not imperial animals or naked apes, bound to the slow and random mutations which produce the stuff for physical evolution. Darwinian we may be in our bodies like the rest of the animal kingdom, but we are Lamarckian in our minds, for we are capable of rearing children who can profit by our lived experience, by mutations recorded not in the genetic code, but in our continuing and collective memories. We have escaped from the prison of instincts that binds our animal cousins, first by our ability to structure and re-structure the world around us through the instruments of our thoughts and, second, because we are able to speak to others and thus to break down the isolation of the individual mind within its brain-cage. In the human, social world, we cannot be only selves, for that world is held together by the fact that we know and communicate with each other, and this we do through our representations, our images, the aspect of the self that is seen and recognized by the other inhabitants of our world.

Let us think of images, then, not just as expressive of the self, but as communications, as messages to other selves. The image which is not the self, but which passes for it in public, fixes the self in social reality because it can be recognized. What I am saying is that the confusion with which I began my thinking on this question is in fact part of the question. For we cannot cut ourselves off from the images others bestow on us even when they seem false to us. Unless those others who share the world with us can point to an image which represents the selves we are, they cannot see us at all. And without this label of image, the self becomes a jibbering ghost, immured in its watch tower, unable to reach the world. Self and image are not the same, but they cannot live apart from each other. Each acts continually on the other in a constant tension, for while the private self is the only source of authentic experience, this experience can only be stated and understood through the public image; and we are, in a way, dependent on being understood to value for ourselves the experience we have known.

To women the valuation of others has come to seem false in terms of our experience; but we cannot simply turn away from the false image without paying a price, the price of alienation. By withdrawing behind the image and nursing the secret self, women have left the false images in command and control. Now, such a withdrawal is natural enough in creatures who have been taught that passivity is proper to them while the attempt to exercise power is not. Perhaps I should pause to remark that I mean it is natural as a learned response of the weak to the powerful whatever sex the weak may have been born with, and not as an innate, genetic mark of femininity. Men who have been born into a status of dependence have found themselves fighting as hard as women to overcome the learned response of passivity and servility. The Black men demanding Black Power today remember the Uncle Toms of the past all too well, remember the entertainers and jokesters and flatterers who survived by amusing, pleasing and toadying to the powerful. They are striving now to wipe that shadow of the phantom slave out of the backgrounds of their minds. Like them, we have learned passivity and the behavior proper to weakness and have learned, with these attitudes, to disvalue ourselves. Perhaps we hug these selves to us as treasures because they are the only things we can call our own. At the same time, we ask ourselves, Who are we to judge comparative values? If these are our treasures, if we take ourselves so seriously, when so obviously the world does not— isn't that just another sign of our foolishness? And consequently isn't it another reason for sitting still in our woman's place and minding our manners, holding our peace, making do with what we know but never say?

That may have been so once, my dear Crazy Jane sisters, but it is so no longer. Like the men who shout that "Black is beautiful," it is time for us to change our images by speaking out. We have withdrawn too long into a private world and by so doing have refused to vivify the image of woman with the authentic pulse and breath of women's lives. The result is a disastrous spate of false images, of cheats which are cheats for men too, which fail even in the social world, so that public reality itself is coming unstuck. The traditional images had some dignity at least, some "redeeming social value," to quote the old Supreme Court on permissible pornography, but these have degenerated into bloodless mechanical puppets. They represent not loving women, but Bunnies for Playboys; not laughing, energetic mothers capable of teaching daughters and sons the ways of the world, but frightened, clutching Moms; not venturesome young explorers, but resentful daughters finding no values in a plastic world to replace the plastic values they have rejected. Because women have let the false images stand as our representatives, we have falsified ourselves, diminished ourselves, chosen to divide ourselves and exist in a hopeless, endless stasis, unable either to act truly or to be ourselves in freedom and enjoyment.

What can we do? We must change our image instead of merely withdrawing inside it and denying that it represents the self. Now I think this can be done, but in the discussions we will be holding here I hope we will recognize both the difficulties inherent in such a change and the opportunities which have newly arisen to make the change possible. Though we are met to talk about the connection and mutual influence of women and the arts, I am going to ask you first to listen to a few dicta from my alter ego, the social historian, for women today occupy a place that is quite new. For the first time in history, social change is altering our experience faster than that of men.

We all know these changes but unless we have put them together we may not realize how extraordinary they are. Let's list a few. Item: we can choose when and whether to have children. Because we can, most of us will outlive the period in which we are involved in active child-rearing by something like half our lives. Item: more and more of us not only know we can earn a living, we are doing so, and planning to do so. Only twenty-five years ago Talcott Parsons, the dean of American sociology, wrote that the choice of a husband was far and away the most important decision that a woman ever made. It's still important, but it's not the only vital decision for women today. Vital too is the choice of vocation; and the certainty that without a husband we can still look after ourselves also influences the husband-choice. We no longer need to grab the first man who proposes or face a life as an old-maid aunt. Just because we don't have to fold our hands and wait for Mr. Right, we do in fact wait for Mr. Right more readily.

At the same time that social change has given us these freedoms, it has taken some away. Item: women who work, whether out of choice or out of need, face a bind that was rarer for their mothers and grand-

12

mothers. The extended family, the close neighborhood, the supportive community, the possibility of good and loving domestic help in raising children, are gone. The motherhood years may be shorter than they used to be, but they are often busier and more hectic and wearing. Item: social mobility picks up families and puts them down a thousand miles from home and roots. At the very time they need more community support, they are getting less.

Then there are changes which don't simply alter our traditional roles, but make them specifically more like those of men. Item: the educations we can get and the work we can do after we get them are more and more similar to men's. Which means that our experience of life is growing closer to that of men, so that the identities we learn from our everyday living may be more like those of our brothers and husbands than they have been in the past. Again, these similarities can be bad as well as good. The work-identities we achieve can be broken off and fragmented by technological obsolescence as much as men's can.

Overall, however, there is a powerful positive value in these shifts. They can be extremely upsetting *but* the future shock we are living with is a force that tells us we must change the old roles and the old image. History may be dragging us by the scruff of the neck into the future—but it is on our side once we realize the need for change. Even inflation is on the side of change. The two-income family is becoming a necessity at many levels of society. Social historians are well aware, even the MCPs among them, that women have worked throughout the centuries at many a difficult and laborious task, but in the past they have been able to do this work largely within the bosom of the family, on the subsistence farm or in the family work-shop. Today we live in a cash economy, and women who work get paid. Now, there are certainly higher and more spiritual values in life than a pay-check, but it's remarkable how much easier it is to think of them once one has got a pay-check in the pocket, and the spiritual value of freedom becomes conceivable.

There is one more point to be made in the historical context. Social change is shaking up not only the lives of women, but the structure of the world around us. For us, change is needed. It may also be easier than ever before because old shibboleths have lost their validity and old processes of life have been drained away. That is often a loss and an impoverishment, but it loosens bonds that have been restrictive too. Consequently, when we think of changing roles and images today, we are much less wishful than we were even fifty years ago. I want to dwell on this point for a moment, because nobody is going to work hard to change anything unless there exists some feeble chance of success. The first feminist wave, which achieved the vote for women, was probably the first generation that could have done it. Technology was giving some women the leisure to fight for more than a living, higher education was giving some women a chance to seize opportunities and others to imagine that their ambitions could be fulfilled and—on the negative side—the factory system was pooling women together and subjecting them to the same pressures in the same place at the same time. The pressures and the opportunities together, plus, remember always, the loosening of social context created by the First World War and the draft of men to fight, bonded women together enough to win our first big victory.

Then, like God on the seventh day, we all sat down and rested for a while. That lull between the first and the second waves of feminism will be a fascinating period to explore some day. Here, let me just say that I believe we were waiting until women's lived experience again changed enough to force another effort on us, while at the same time, the historical context produced the opportunities for change to come. That has happened now, and that is where we are today. So I shall say farewell for the moment to history and return to the topic of our conference.

But I hope you will understand why I have made this digression when I say that I believe the only way we can create a new and valid image of woman is out of our lived experience, our confrontation with history. That experience has always modified the stereotypes of sex and class. In the past, however, personal life and public life ran closer together. Big families and small communities where men and women lived close to their roots guaranteed that people knew each other well over long stretches of their lives. Stereotypes of behavior certainly existed, but they were continually being adjusted to match the personalities of people whom one knew in an intimate, long-term way. Think of Chaucer's women, think of Shakespeare's. Over and over vivid, speaking reality bursts through the image to illuminate it with immediate reactions to everyday life. Which means that if we call on the resources of the self and its felt experience to help us create a new image, we are following a known path.

Today, however, we must do it more consciously and on a grander scale. And here, I think, we come right to the heart of the matter of our meeting, to the connection between women and the arts. For I believe that the way we use personal experience to create a new image of woman is closely allied to the work of the artist. Within art we can find the finished creations of the insightful mind which will act as guides to the future, and that is a great deal. But even more vital, we can find in art the very process of creativity itself which we shall be using to reshape our image. For art is the way in which internal experience is formed into the image which is comprehensible to others. It is a basic process of communication, which establishes for one human being the interior reality, the lived experience of another; and this is what is demanded of us today.

Let me say that in formulating this definition of art and of creativity I am indebted to a very great philosopher who happens to be a woman, Susanne Langer. She is also the only philosopher of art of whom I know who is read with passion and delight by practising artists: writers, musicians and painters have all told me so. In her book, *Feeling and Form,* Langer offers a simple definition of art. It is, she says, "the creation of forms symbolic of human feeling." Again, in a later work, *Mind: An Essay on Human Feeling,* she writes: "Artistic conception . . . is not a transitional phase of mental evolution, but a final symbolic form making revelation of truths about actual life." (p. 81, vol. I.) And these truths are communicable. I quote again: "(The artist) creates an image of that phase of events which only the organism wherein they occur

ever knows. This image, however, serves two purposes in human culture, one individual, and one social: it articulates our own life of feeling so that we become conscious of its elements and its intricate and subtle fabric, and it reveals the fact that the basic forms of feeling are common to most people at least within a culture, and often far beyond it. . . Art is the surest affidavit that feeling, despite its absolute privacy, repeats itself in each individual life." (p. 64.) It is, moreover, the only form of communication which can convey the truths of internal feelings. "The facts which it makes conceivable are precisely those which literal statement distorts." (p. 81.)

In creating a new image, then, we shall have to proceed as if we were artists. For us, art is both guide and paradigm. I hope that isn't a frightening idea. It shouldn't be. Creativity is not really a rare gift, it is just one that we have rather systematically pushed out of our lives for a while. But it is present not just in the high arts of music and drama and dance and literature and painting and sculpture, it is present in folk art too. The quilts our great-grandmothers made, the knitting patterns they adapted, the embroidery with which they enlivened simple traditional styles of clothing, were all products of creativity. So were folk songs and work songs and country dances, weaving and pottery making and all the crafts that were in earlier days a necessary part of life. We haven't lost the ability to create just because we've let it slide: creativity is one thing human beings are born with. And since we also possess the capacity to learn, we can re-learn and re-use old skills, the skills which show us how to transmute the feeling of life into the expressive image which will represent us truly in the social, human world.

How do we begin? First, before everything, by listening to ourselves, listening to our experience as an artist listens to a work that is trying to be born; by listening deeply and listening humbly, but with a sense of trust and confidence that we can understand what our experience shows we require, for that is what the new image must incorporate. Let me emphasize that element of confidence, for the old image of woman is going to rise at once to dispute it; and the old image of woman, of the good woman,

14

Gwen. Photo by Judy Dater (San Anselmo, Cal.), 1972.

is still far from dead. She is still very influential, still felt by many of us to be an important and proper model when she tells us that our central characteristic is devotion to others and that our very capacity for feeling—which we are trying to use for our own ends in remaking our image—is misused unless we forget *our* feelings and put others first.

But that is what we cannot do as creators. The image of the good woman is thoroughly ambivalent, which is to say that there are indeed still valuable elements within it; that we do certainly want to be open to others and receptive and giving in personal relationships. But we must be more. The old model of the good woman has become insufficient for life today, and it is especially inappropriate in the struggle for the expression of experience that we face in creating the new image which will enlarge the old. The old image has grown so small and so narrow that it has cut out a whole range of feeling and by so doing, it makes our responses smaller and less valuable than they should be. Let us put the old image gently aside and see ourselves not as good *women*, but as good *artists*, for the job we are tackling is simply a larger, social form of the artist's work. And every artist knows that an intuitive sense of the reality and the worth of others must be matched with a kind of sublime faith in one's own ability to conceive a new truth and embody it in the right, revealing symbols, a faith which at times approaches arrogance. If a writer, painter, composer, doesn't know what is true and necessary in his vision and isn't prepared to hold on to that knowledge in the teeth of everyone else's opinion, he had better go into some other business. Equally, if women are not prepared to believe that they understand their own lives better than do men, they will not have the courage and stamina to change them. And change them we must.

So, we listen. And one of the people we listen to is certainly Crazy Jane. She is a good antidote to the old model of the good woman and her obligatory dedication to others. Jane will tell us to beware of old ideas, most notably the idea that women are possessed of finer, nobler, less aggressive and more nurturant qualities than men. Not only can no one prove that, the mere

existence of the belief is hampering to women. It invites a sort of emotional snobbery, akin to the intellectual snobbery which blinds those who suffer from it to new ideas because they are so sure they know best that they don't have to listen. But we have to listen and we have to look, with Jane's cold eye, at all the experience we have turned our backs on in the past because it wasn't proper for good women. We have a great deal to learn about coping with man's world. For instance I am sure we need to know more about the positive value of aggression, and stubbornness, and decisiveness, and daring, when these qualities are called for. They happen to be called for now, because they are the qualities that allow the artist to control the stuff he is working with.

We must not be put off by the idea that these qualities are selfish. So they are, in a special, a primary way: it is ourselves which we must be willing to explore in our search for the true experience we must use in our creative task. But this selfishness is quite different from the selfishness that is a product of vicarious living. That sort is exclusive, possessive, mean-minded. It says, if I can't have the world, if I can't reach for what I need, then I'll snatch at what's left, I'll take this and hold it so tightly that no one can share.

Primary selfishness, on the other hand, is for sharing because it is based on enjoyment, on one's own enjoyment, not simply a reaction to the enjoyment of others. It is a form of self-enrichment. Women very much need to know what pleases them immediately, because our enjoyment has been filtered through others for so long. We are pleased at being thought well of: at wolf-whistles on the street, or five invitations for Saturday night, or the symbols of celebrity, our name on an office door. These things are not what I mean when I say we will find out who we are, and therefore how our image should be shaped, by discovering enjoyment. I mean a sense of connection with the world, and pleasure flowing from the world, and discrimination about that pleasure even as you feel it; so that you hear music that turns the world to gold, remember it, and know whose it is; know whose poetry explodes in your head, whose books ride with you through life as guides and comforters. I mean what paintings and sculptures you call on when you come back to Paris or Athens or Basel or Washington or Boston, what makes you laugh and equally what doesn't. I mean what sports you love, for they partake of the esthetic qualities we assign too narrowly to high art. I mean the pleasures of good food and fine weather and the rise and fall of certain landscapes and animals moving and children on a beach, and half a hundred things more at least, things that color the world and teach us to discriminate.

To discriminate, again, on our own, so that it is our own personal experience that tells us what is pleasant and what is painful, for it is only by learning this *on our own* that we can trust ourselves to discriminate further, so that we go on, with equal confidence to say, this is good and that is bad, this is just and that is oppression, this is true and that is false. We need to know these things for ourselves and not through mediators, because we must trust ourselves and our knowledge. That trust, that confidence, is the instrument of the creator, and no one can work without it.

But this immediate, discriminating knowledge of the validity of experience is also the ground beneath the social structure. Our image is not for ourselves alone, it is a message, a communication of truth. Our society is in bad trouble today because too many messages have been falsified, too few of us rely on our experience to validate our lives. Let me remind you of a recent example of what I'm talking about from a field quite apart from art, or from women either. Do you remember when Sam Ervin was asked, during the Watergate hearings, by someone, Ehrlichmann's lawyer, I think, how he—Ervin, that is—knew what Section so-and-so of Title this-or-that of the Criminal Code meant, and Ervin answered in utter astonishment, "How do I know? Because I understand the English language. It's my mother tongue."

Now, Senator Ervin did not mean that he was born knowing English. Like all of us, he learned his mother-tongue. So let us note, at once, that this intuitive, subliminal knowledge *can be learned*. Once learned, this immediacy, developed through a life-time of connection and response, is the way that the self knows valid experience. Experience is our mother-tongue; but if we are to trust it, we must be open to it ourselves, take it in by ourselves, and not through mediators.

And if we are going to change the false image which represents women to the world, this sort of trust in what we know and feel, this responsiveness which doesn't quibble about how we know at the moment of knowledge, which uses the self by forgetting the self, is the fundamental means through which we can do our work. It is just here that we shall find the touchstone of authenticity which will help us in this formidable task. We cannot undertake to change our image in any half-hearted way, distracted by caveats from the past, from the old assigned image. We shall have to engage the individual personalities of hundreds, thousands, millions of women, each of whom will know the necessity of the task within herself. What we have on our side is already the statement by history that it is necessary, that social change demands it. But if we are to create not just a different, but a true image we need more than the knowledge of necessity. We need the motivation of joy in creation, of delight and connection with life. We need more than a push from history, we need a pull from the possible future.

The creative process, implicit in art, can help us imagine that future, can help us test it against our own actual experience and then, by showing us the reality of other human feelings, embodied in art, it can extend our experience, so that we know we do not speak for the odd, individual self alone. In art, the self speaks through the image *and is recognized.* Crazy Jane, so long alone, will finally find her name; and in so doing she will become more than the cold, passive observer. Because she is recognizable, because singular experience has been transformed into an image which can be shared and understood, the image affects the interior lives of its audience until they become—Jane and all of us, or the Jane in all of us—not just audience, but participants. This is the task we are undertaking today, the creation of a true symbol of ourselves out of our special, lived experience which will explain our identities, both to others and to ourselves. We shall find ourselves here, just as the artist finds, as he finishes his work, what the work means and says. Let me say again, art is a guide for us not just to the image, but to the making of the image; and the making will shape the image for we shall learn, as we work, who we are. The process will tell us what the symbol must be, for the very work itself will enlarge and enrich the image we are making. We must live not just as women, but as artists, open and daring but always alive to our own experience, listening and assertive both, trying out our new-found voices but knowing, as we do, that the music we are making will not be just ours, but that of a great chorus.

One last word. Last year I found myself asked why a group of women, of whom I was one, had discussed the place of women in the world and the significance of women's experience and, as we did so, had referred to women not as "we" but as "they." I think there were many reasons for this. One of them was certainly that we all happened to be writers, and writers tend to keep a distance between themselves and their work (*their* work, you see, not *our* work. I don't fall into this distancing only in speaking of women. Writers do that because this distance imposes impersonality and keeps individual crankiness from getting in the way of abstraction. But another reason, I felt, was that for me, at any rate, there is a larger "we" than women. That "we" is humankind.

I bring this up because I think it is important for us to realize how vital a new image of women is for humanity as a whole. We live in a divided society. Art and feeling have both been assigned to women.

Dealing with practical events has been reserved for men, and has thus been separated from the expression of feeling. And now we are discovering the price exacted for that division—I mean "we" there, I mean humankind. The western world is sick with a great malaise that stems from this division. You can find it in the disturbing statistics on job alienation, with their evidence of working men and working women who go to their jobs in a spirit of disgust and boredom and hate. You can see it reflected in the determined refusal of young people to project lives conforming to the traditional ideals of western society, of respect for work, the system, the country where one was born. All the old patterns of life that should be familiar and sustaining have come to seem a cheap, mocking show. You can hear it in the defiled language of the Watergate witnesses whose words and grammar and syntax are all intended not to express the truth of authentic experience, but to disguise it, so that they mouth one thing and mean another. And it has happened because the world of events, man's world, has been drained of feeling and has lost, therefore, a sense of the human dimensions of life, both great and small, and of real human requirements.

It is very necessary that this division be healed, so that feeling and action can once more flow together. A new image of woman as active participant in society does not mean that women will desert the emotional validity of personal relations as we move into the world of action. We will bring it along with us, to a place where it is badly needed. □

**NEW IMAGES OF WOMEN:
A RESPONSIBILITY FOR ARTISTS?**

Discussion Leader: May Stevens
Artist and lecturer.

May Stevens: I feel that the artist's responsibility is to make art. There's no other way to make art but honestly. I think that some of the worst art has been created when the artist listened to a politburo, a bureaucrat or to an ideology. On the other hand, I believe that the women's movement is causing a lot of information to come to the

Judith Jamison. Photo by Jack Mitchell. Courtesy: The Alvin Ailey Dance Theatre.

surface which is changing the intellectual climate that we live in. Women are beginning to stop lying about themselves and their experiences; they're beginning to rewrite the history of art. We are going to have a new mass of information which will be controversial and many of our beliefs will have to be amended. All of this will influence the arts produced by men and women.

Linda Nochlin: What if some women want to paint motorcycles? I might want to do a very hard-edged painting with no reference to anything as expressing part of me. Or I might want to do very aggressive things. I might want to do paintings about Vietnam as part of my most deep experience as a woman. Isn't any creation of mythic imagery a kind of group input which says, well, if you're a woman you have to do it like this. How do you break through that?

May Stevens: There is an attitude among *some* women artists which corresponds to what you're suggesting. They feel that if you do hard-edged abstract painting, you are not being a woman, you are being a male follower. They also feel that it's not authentic for a woman to do hard-edged abstract painting and to have precise forms.

I think this is a very dangerous kind of limitation.

Betsy Damon: Women will paint cars when that's their experience—when they work on cars; when they become mechanics.

Linda Nochlin: The interesting anomaly is that women spend more of their lives in cars than many men do. After all, we are the ones who are picking up the kids and so on; we are the ones who do the shopping. Why are men permitted to take cars over as their symbol when really we're the chauffeurs of America? So much mythology is involved in what you take over as your imagery.

Harriet FeBland: It's my experience with women students that they always apologize before they show you anything. Similarly as I meet other women artists and I speak to them, they will apologize before they show me their work. I think it is very sad to find this at the level of professional artists.

Nancy Knaak: Isn't that part of humanity though? I think that if you're going to slap me down I'll protect myself first, and then if it looks like you aren't going to raise your

Sculpter Louise Kruger. Photo by Nina Howell Starr (New York), from her portfolio "Strength of Women."

fist, I have more trust in you and I'm better able to reveal myself.

Linda Nochlin: Men don't. There may be some who are very modest but, having taught both men and women, I find that men are often either more confident or put on a much bolder front than women. Men who are teaching pre-architectural students also feel this is true. They tell me that their women students are actually far superior to the men students but all of them think they're no good. They question how they are going to get into architecture; they are profusely apologetic. Whereas mediocre men students know they're going to be architects; they already consider themselves on a professional level. They'll bluff or bluster through things they don't know or simply stay up all night to learn them. They're much less concerned with their own sensibilities; they'll take hard criticism and bounce back because they know where they're going to go.

Ruth Milofsky: I think both things are facades. I think women may apologize for the purpose of being reassured. I encounter that particularly with beginners or with older women who have gone back to school. I think men's weakness is having to bluster all the time.

May Stevens: Presenting your work with apologies is one way of making sure that you're not going to make it.

Dorothy Austin: Have we decided that the woman artist has a responsibility to women?

Harriet FeBland: Well, a woman artist is not an island. She needs other women. One of

the first things I say in my workshop is that women need women and they should not feel that other women are competition. Competition should be with themselves. The first rule is that you help your fellow women.

Betsy Damon: I think we need other women as critics, as supporters, as teachers. I think we need other women to tell us to be more selfish, to take care of ourselves, and instead of telling us to be better mothers and to be service people, to tell us that we are not service people.

Barbara Coffman: We've gotten away from the question of whether it's important for us to recognize ourselves as a woman artist or an artist.

Harriet FeBland: The responsibility of a woman artist is to be female first and if she is female, she can be true to herself in her art.

Betsy Damon: It's also our responsibility to educate other people and relate to other women.

Linda Nochlin: I feel the ultimate goal is a kind of androgyny. I feel myself to be an androgynous person: my deepest feelings are equally what our culture defines as masculine—very aggressive, energetic, and intellectual. That's just as much part of me, in some ways more a part of me, than the gentle, giving, sexual. In other words, I don't have to distort myself to think of myself in terms of what is considered the conventional woman. Perhaps more and more women are feeling the way I'm feeling. □

IMAGERY IN PUBLIC EDUCATION

Discussion Leader: Gertrude Herman
Associate Professor of Library Science at the University of Wisconsin-Madison.

Gertrude Herman: The question is how can we bring up boys and girls whose inner realities and outer realities are not at war

with each other, but which represent parts of a total personality which, if they become unified, make for a creative experiencing of life in spite of the chaos that surrounds us. How can we produce young people, both boys and girls, who trust themselves and are thus able to use themselves with all their passions and talents and yearnings instead of being frustrated by society? Some of the myths of our sexuality are so deeply ingrained in western culture that I doubt that we can ever really get rid cf them.

I think one of the key questions is: How can we best influence the selection of educational materials which are used on local, state, or national levels? If we use a screening process, who does the screening? Now you're getting on very touchy grounds because there are all kinds of people who would like to screen what children read and what public schools choose in the way of textbooks. Our cause is holy but there are causes which are not so holy. Who decides? Aren't you getting into a kind of censorship when you begin to choose your books in terms of the social message and the approval or the disapproval of the social message?

Theodore Shannon: There is a general unavailability of alternative books as compared to the stereotyped books. The issue is not so much screening the material but making available to receptive people sources of good materials—giving them a chance to discriminate.

Vivienne Anderson: Could I bring up a practical problem related to this issue? In our department we have a task force on equal opportunities for women designated by our Commissioner of Education. This is one of his big priorities and in fact the governor of the state has also just organized a task force on equal opportunities for women. There's going to be a fairly strong movement in this direction throughout the state. How do you influence selection of books and curriculum? What are your standards of criteria and how do you get your decisions put into practice? Now, our task force is working on a couple of different avenues which I will just mention very briefly. One is equal opportunity of employment and status. Another one has to do specifically with focusing on curriculum materials that go out of the State Education Department— any pronouncements, written or oral state-

ments that are made. In other words if you have good books free of stereotypes, what do you do about it? We have the charge of attitudinal change in our highest knowledge area levels of the department because until some kind of change can be effectuated there and commitments are made to a policy of equality you can't accomplish anything in a bureaucracy. The thing I wanted to put on the table was this: if the members of this workshop were a task force working on a statewide level, could we suggest any strategies that might be practical for scrutinizing curricula materials and commercial materials that are disseminated on a statewide basis within school districts?

Cynthia Pitts: I think this is probably the most crucial question that we will be dealing with in any of the workshops. The conference is supposed to form a process for making the rhetoric of a movement actually function. I would imagine that by the time a state task force is established the analysis of the problem has already been done. I would think that what has to be identified is: What are the formal structures where those decisions which will be utilized by the task force are made? The other questions that state, private groups, and public groups have to deal with are: What resources are they going to allocate to tne implementation of a plan? For example, if you're talking about curriculum, will they hire a person to do the content analysis or will this same group just break down into sub-groups to do it? If so, are they going to have the time it takes to get the work done? What are the resources of an institution? And what are the mechanisms for decision-making? Who makes them and what is the commitment to getting things done? It is a very difficult thing to change attitudes. You have to have people in positions of influence whose interests are served through the kind of change that we are talking about. Then they have to negotiate and lobby at the level where they are. Hence, you're talking about women in major decision-making roles as opposed to members of a task force who come up with a very good idea and then submit it somewhere where there is no one to represent that interest and carry it through. This is a problem in all the humanistic movements—how do you get programs implemented and maintained?

Gertrude Herman: You could almost change your words and say civil rights or any minority groups would be faced with the same strategy problems—money, power, and, of course, attitudes. There has been a tremendous amount of groundwork already done as you have so wisely pointed out. It is encouraging, however, that there has been research and there have been societal changes. Everything that has gone on in the last five years in the women's movement has begun to educate people and sensitize them to this problem.

Jean Cronan: I would like to speak to her question as a parent who has been a member of a curriculum advisory committee. I was chosen as a parent to be on a book selection committee in the Madison Public School System. They were trying to pick an American History book for ninth grade which, of course, has traditionally been the year in which history was not taught. The reason they chose me was because my husband happens to be an historian. I laughed about that but I thought I could do my homework and here was a chance to do something. On the committee we had a person interested in black history to make sure that the history in the ninth-grade texts would represent blacks; we had women trying to make sure that the feminist viewpoint was represented; and there were many teachers. We had stacks of textbooks to go through, and I would come home to read them and take notes. We would all come back to the meetings—to what we hoped would be meaningful discussions—but the meetings deteriorated to the point where the educators had to be called back with all their jargon to help us solve the problem. I have to say that after meeting weekly for six months, we found that there weren't many books published for ninth graders in American history. Most of them were for older or younger students. And second, most of the teachers had the opportunity to do what they wanted to anyway. We could choose a book, but they wouldn't use it. I thought it was a waste of my time.

Gertrude Herman: I want to raise one word of caution. When you get into book selection committees of lay people you are get-ting into very touchy ground, and you may be releasing something that you may not want to release. For example, in California, there has been a tremendous conflict over whether the book of Genesis should be taught on an equal level with the theory of evolution. There are many fundamentalists in California and they almost succeeded in pushing through the California schools that you had to teach the story of the creation of the world in six days as being as equally possible a theory as the theory of evolution. There is a big conflict over a children's book called *Sylvester and the Magic Pebble* because it is a book about animals and in that book the policeman was pictured as a pig. Policemen associations all over the country were up in arms. And that book got withdrawn from the Toledo public schools. We have a cause and we know it is a good one but others think that their cause is also good.

Theodore Shannon: I think the lack of teaching materials is a very critical one. I blame it on the teaching profession, I blame it on the librarians, I blame it on the people who don't put pressure on the publishing houses. Nothing moves publishing houses like dollars. And it's easy to pressure publishing houses. It's ironic that the only place in the publishing world where women have any clout is in the children's literature department. I think we ought to be working on upper management in the publishing houses not only on the children's literature.

Gertrude Herman: It's interesting to note that the juvenile department often is the money maker for the senior department.

Cynthia Pitts: I want to say a little more about lay people's advisory structures and the risk involved in this kind of policy making. If you believe in freedom of expression then you believe that the person who wants to teach evolution or Genesis as factually correct has the right to be heard but he doesn't have the right to dictate. You need an equal and fair expression of many opinions. If you really do believe your cause is a good one, then you have to see to it that you begin to move into the power structure and the decision-making levels. ☐

INNER REALITY OF WOMEN

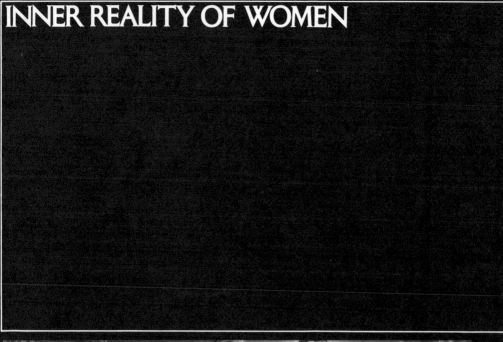

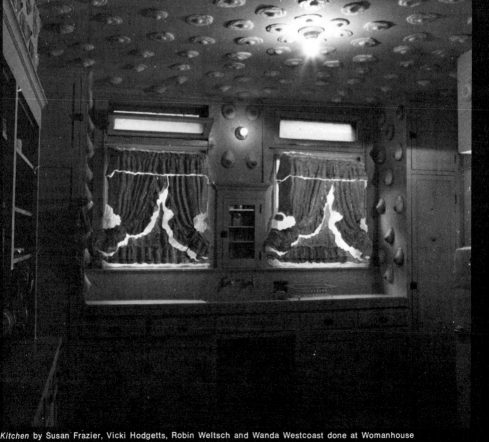

Kitchen by Susan Frazier, Vicki Hodgetts, Robin Weltsch and Wanda Westcoast done at Womanhouse in connection with The California Institute of the Arts' Feminist Art Program.

by Ravenna Helson
*Institute of Personality Assessment and
Research, University of California-Berkeley.*

A decade ago the subject of a paper like this might well have been, "Why are there no creative women?" And this negatively loaded question would have elicited ready answers. Someone would have quoted Helene Deutsch, explaining that a woman could not develop the requisite masculine traits of assertiveness, concentration on work, etc., without repressing her feminine nature and her originality along with it. Esther Harding would have suggested that women are naturally personal and modest and that drawing attention to one's own creation means exposing one's deepest feeling and that this would arouse defensive processes which would defeat the attempt at communication. Carl Pribam would have asked: How could there be a creative woman? We might try to make a girl creative, but it would be an agonizing process, if not impossible, because it would mean making a man of her in the best sense of the word.

Today there are still voices which carry a similar message. In her pioneering book, *The Psychology of Women* (1972), Judith Bardwick says: ". . . the greater creativity of the boy is easily observed even in the lower school grades."

But we have learned a lot about the social context of creativity. For example, Linda Nochlin has pointed out that very few first-rank artists have come from the aristocracy; yet we assume not that aristocrats lack the little golden nugget of creativity but that their way of life precluded serious commitment to a career as an artist. And so it has been with women through most of human history. The pattern of life established by child-bearing and child-rearing precluded their serious commitment to art. Today, however, women have a new way of life. The population explosion has made it imperative that women have fewer children and the contraceptive revolution has made it possible for them to do so. As Margaret Mead and others have said, "Women are about to be freed from their slavery to biology."

Without disagreeing with this evaluation we

25

may still examine the other side of the coin. The oldest known sculptures show a fertility goddess. Mary is queen in heaven, which she is because she was the mother of Jesus. Woman's biological creativity and her role as mother are what have given women their importance throughout most of human history. If these roles are devalued in the interest of controlling population, what do women have left?

Certainly woman's role as worker has taken on a new importance. About 40% of the labor force is female; however, women participate at a low status level. They are paid less than men and they are concentrated in work which consists of performing services for others. We have no image of women as creative in the world of work.

One might think that it would be easy to move from the idea of woman as creator of children to the idea of woman as creator of ideas but this does not seem to be an easy transfer. One reason for this is that scientists, including psychologists, usually think of creativity in terms of a phallocentric male model, such as the problem-solving paradigm. There is a goal to be reached with a barrier in the way; one tries to identify the barrier, bypass it and penetrate to the solution. If one thinks in terms of this male model, the idea of a creative woman is awkward. The emphasis is on such traits as forcefulness, achievement orientation, speed of reaction, in which men tend to excel. One tends to ignore the female contribution to procreation. Sometimes people do describe creativity in part in terms of the female procreative model— common expressions are to conceive an idea, to have a brainchild, etc. And yet these terms are not regarded as particularly appropriate for women. It is the creative male who is described as bisexual, especially in the arts, and these terms are appropriate for him. The woman's place is in the real world, not the intellectual world of speculation and possibility. Her function is to contain, to conserve, and not to initiate. Long ago in a battle between patriarchal and matriarchal points of view, Apollo said:

Fred's Magic Die-Box, lithograph from *Wonder Production*, Volume I, by Ellen Lanyon (Chicago).

*Not the mother is the creatress of the
  child
She only bears and nurtures awakened
  life.
The father creates; she keeps the fruit
As a favor for her friend, if no god
  intercedes.*

It is easy to form a similar idea today, that
men do all that is important even in physical childbirth. One man puts a seed in the
hat, and another takes the rabbit out.
Although the patriarchal domination of
procreation is being challenged on various
levels, the voice of Apollo is still loud in
our land.

As the psychology of prejudice would lead
us to expect, evidence that does not fit the
image of woman as container and supporter
tends to be ignored or distorted. A good
example is the school book presentation of
Florence Nightingale. This forceful and
original action-researcher usually appears
in a white nightgown with the caption,
"Florence Nightingale comforted the
wounded."

Let us look briefly at several aspects of the
social context which determine whether
women become artists and how they perform in that role. This is a bit of concentration on Outer Realities before going more
into Inner Realities. Artists are not selected
and processed in as obvious a way as
dentists, lawyers or boilermakers, but they
are recruited nonetheless. Teachers, for
example, are important, picking out certain
children for special attention, calling on
them to tell a story, sending them to a
special class, entering them in a contest, or
in other ways preparing them to think of
themselves as potential artists. Not much
is known about which children are selected
and which overlooked, but we have some
evidence that teachers reward originality in
boys and compliance in girls. A number of
studies suggest that girls, more than boys,
need the advantages of privileged social
class and educated and enlightened
parents.

Several studies have compared men and
women in art school. Barron and his colleagues found some dramatic differences at
the San Francisco Art Institute. Though the
men and women did not differ in the quality
of their work as rated by the art school
faculty, there were large differences in the
way they talked about their work and
planned their future careers. For example,
to the question, "Do you think of yourself
as an artist?" most of the women said *no*
(67 percent) but most of the men said *yes*
(66 percent). The men already thought of
themselves as artists, where the women
viewed themselves as "student artists perhaps—but not artists, not yet."

Forty percent of the men thought their work
was superior in comparison to others at the
art school and only fourteen percent
thought their work was inferior. The per-
centages were almost reversed for women:
only seventeen percent thought their work
was superior and almost forty percent considered it inferior. The men frequently made
statements such as: "Painting is my life,"
and "If I couldn't paint, I would rather die."
Women were much more guarded or tentative—certainly less passionate: "I'm not
sure yet, but I like it," "It's half my life, the
other half is my future family." These
results are all the more striking when you
consider that women art students are
reported to be more masculine than other
women, more confident, verbally aggressive,
etc. These statements suggest a very
strange tentativeness in certain areas of
career commitment.

A factor which needs to be taken into
account is that men in art school have been
preselected more than the women. The
dramatic clash between aspiring male
artists and their parents takes place *before*
the decision to go to art school. Thus the
men are already committed, but the women
have not made any equivalent controversial
decision—against marriage or children,
for example.

But, of course, more men than women do
have a strong commitment to work.
Barron's very striking material is registering
the effects of different cultural expectations
for men and women—that the man should
express himself in work and should aim for
the highest he can achieve, that the woman
should devote herself to her husband and
family and should be modest in her personal apirations. If she departs from these
expectations, she is likely to be unsure of
herself and cautious in exposing herself to
social censure or retaliation.

It is thus understandable that strength of commitment to work is a factor which powerfully distinguishes creative women from other women. Among both the mathematicians and writers that I have studied, the single self-descriptive statement which most strongly differentiated the more creative from the less creative or "comparison" women was this: "Subordinates other things to research (or literary) goals; puts these values before others." Creative women are not as likely to express a desire to dominate a field or to achieve immortality as men. Perhaps they have less hope of it, perhaps they are hesitant to admit such ambition, or perhaps the desire for fame is not as important to them. But we cannot compare men and women in too simple-minded a way. Certainly, the creative women do not lack motivation. They manifest it in the "purity" of their lives, for example, in the number of extraneous activities that they are willing to give up in the interests of their work.

In studying mathematicians and authors, I found that men and women mathematicians were much more different from each other in personality than men and women writers, who were quite similar. Where the creative women mathematicians were very low on Self-Acceptance, the creative male mathematicians differed from them and from both the men and women writers in their social assertiveness and conventional attitudes towards achievement (relative to comparison subjects). Although several factors may contribute to this pattern, one obvious fact is that the creative male mathematicians were alone in having a secure and prestigious institutional status. They were professors at distinguished institutions. But more than one-third of the creative women mathematicians in the country had no regular jobs at all and only two or three of them taught graduate students. Institutions have almost always organized women "out" or "under." One reason that women have excelled in literature is that it is the field freest from institutional regulation. And yet women have prospered in a friendly small-group atmosphere—one thinks of Margaret Fuller, Harriet Mill, Maria Edgeworth, Virginia Woolf, etc. Unfortunately women artists do not often seem to find such an atmosphere. Barron had the strong impression that the San Francisco Art Institute faculty did not take women students seriously. He quotes this as a typical faculty remark: "They may hang on and graduate but all they ever do then is teach school or get married or get a job doing something else. They never have a one-man show, never, not one in the whole history of the school." The art faculty seems to have little insight or interest about why the women's record looks like this.

Several years ago Bernard Rosenberg and Norris Fliegel wrote in *The Vanguard Artist:* "When the woman artist complains that it is difficult for her to gain a foothold in the art world, she's not simply being paranoid. For all her achievements, she must be prepared to deal with bias, prejudice, or outright hostility—and it emanates from many sources." Gallery owners, dealers, museum directors include many who are prejudiced against women. But the group who may hurt the most are the women artists' male peers. Of twenty-two male artists interviewed by Rosenberg and Fliegel, twenty-one said that women artists were trying to prove they were men, that they were aggressive, imitative—and if not imitative, that they worked in a feminine style inferior to that of men—and were not interesting as women or as people.

Exploring male attitudes towards achievement in women, Pleck and Tresemer have recently described two syndromes which they call *stereotyping* and *hostile resistance.* The stereotyping syndrome seems to be found in men who are high in ego strength and are strong achievers. Such a man is chivalrous and feels sure that a woman would find her happiness in his strength; in playing a role complementary to his. He doesn't find women a threat to his status as an achiever but he is dependent on them, although he doesn't think of it quite that way, for emotional support and expression. We recognize this type, but it is the second syndrome that may apply better to male artists. These men are weaker in ego strength and less sure of themselves as achievers. They may have a history of struggle against female authority. They are quick to perceive women as competitors and to perceive all women as aggressive and as wanting to dominate any situation they can. Studies of art students seem to agree that the men are more "feminine" than the norm and that women are more "masculine"—have more initiative, more verbal aggression and are more adventurous. So the situation seems to be that many aspiring women in art have characteristics to which the male ingroup shows hostile resistance.

We have been talking about some of the outer realities that women face—the social expectation that they will devote themselves foremost to a family, and the assumption that since this is the case, they cannot be taken seriously; the social dogma that man is the innovator and woman the conserver; the damaging prejudices within the art establishment. These outer realities can cause confusion, conflict, and self-doubt when they clash with a woman's sense of a different "inner reality." Though we are talking about women artists in particular, we are also concerned with a problem that afflicts a much larger group.

I would like to discuss four attitudes toward the inner and outer realities among some women I have studied. The women are authors of fantasy for children. Fantasy for children is a rather special genre, and one most interesting for our purpose because it tends especially to attract individuals who want to work through and express a sense of selfhood. They may not be writing for children at all, but in our society that is where fantasy, especially if there is cheer or constructiveness in it, gets marketed. This body of writing seems to be relevant to us in our concern with the efforts of women artists to achieve their own image and to help other women to do the same. The syndromes that I am going to describe can be regarded as self-portraits, as integrative styles which can be found in areas other than literary fantasy for children and at times other than the present.

My study began with a systematic description of books written since 1930 for children of ages eight to twelve. Later the authors were asked to participate in an investigation of relationships between personality and creative product. More than eighty percent of the authors who were still alive and English-speaking agreed to participate. We have also studied books from the nineteenth century with the same questionnaire that was used to describe the contemporary fantasy.

Adoption of Outer Reality

I asked the writers to describe their way of working by ranking a set of fifty-six items or statements that had to do with various aspects of work style. A cluster analysis of these data showed that certain groups of items tended to vary together. One of these clusters was as follows:

+ Money is an important motivating factor.
+ Would welcome adoption of work by the mass media.
+ Can work under an editor.
+ Writes for reader rather than for self.
− Subordinates other things to literary goals.
− Is aware of personality changes related to work.

The pluses and minuses indicate that writers who put the plus items high tend to put the minus items low, and vice versa. If money is an important motivating factor, if they hope to get on the Walt Disney show and so forth, then they do *not* subordinate other things to literary goals and they do *not* experience personality changes related to their work.

Women who score high on this cluster show also on personality tests and in response to interview questions that they are very sensitive to external demands and rewards. Their books are not rated high on creativity, but they may be quite lively and popular. These women tend not only to adopt the feminine role, but to identify with it and use it in their work. In stories for children, the central character is often a clever woman who copes with bad children, helpless parents, or a weak husband. The story may be sentimental, suspenseful, or humorous; whichever it is, the author is manipulating our emotions for maximum effect. Inner life is usually not highly developed in these women, because they are too interested in social roles and social success.

This type of author has been around a long time. An illustration from a children's book of the nineteenth century captures the spirit of her fantasy; it shows several weeping men, heads bowed, standing or kneeling around a figure on what is clearly a death bed. On the wall, in the center of the picture, hangs a large portrait of a mother and child.

We may feel some ambivalence towards this type of author. She is the typical "lady novelist" of best sellers. But, in a period when the feminine role is on the upgrade, she may play a progressive part, especially in winning support from conservative segments of society. This seems to have been true of the sentimental novelists before the Civil War. These women were very interested in the changing feminine role of the time. They often depicted exciting, emotional stereotypes, but many of them were feminists and they got in a lot of "good licks" for the cause of women.

Concentration on the Inner Reality

Another type of woman pays only nominal attention to the outer realities. She may even be outspoken in her contempt for them, not particularly as they relate to the feminine role but as they relate to humanity. Socially, she may see herself as unfriendly, preoccupied, self-centered, gauche, as a "Crazy Jane." She doesn't believe in cleverness or in being busy and active, but rather in attunement to nature and inner life. These women are almost the opposite of the first group. If you ask an author who is adapted to the feminine role and to outer adjustment how she came to write a certain book, she may say, "Well, my first book was such a success and I didn't want to be labeled a one-book writer or a writer of horse stories, so I dug out this old theme that always went over big whenever I used it in school and I added a love interest and did this or that for suspense." Her account is about *doing* things in order to get a certain *effect* from the audience. But the author of the second type may say, "It just wrote itself;" and if you want to know a little more than that, she might say, "Well, I really don't like to pry into it." But then you find that it was a special time in her life; she had left her home town, perhaps she had an unbelievable love affair, with the mood lingering; and then one day she found herself writing about this strange character or this strange place. In the books written by these women, mood or setting is very important—forests, fogs, old houses and gardens. Often there

From *Misunderstood* by Florence Montgomery.

From *Mary Poppins Opens the Door* by P. L. Travers, copyright 1943, 1971. Illustration by Mary Shepard and Agnes Sims. Reprinted by permission of Harcourt Brace Jovanovich, Inc.

is a magical woman—a grandmother or godmother. The author is interested in bringing feelings into the right relationship —not under the rule of a king, as might be the male way, but in a natural order.

The woman who was rendered as a picture on the wall by the first type of author becomes spiritualized, an inner figure, in the works of this second type. *The Tapestry Room* by the nineteenth-century English author, Mrs. Molesworth, illustrates these various characteristics: strange unreal settings, a mysterious spinning woman who tells a boy-girl pair the story of "The Brown Bull of Norroway," an account of the personality development of a young woman through her encounters with the lower and higher masculine principles.

One supposes that the realization of an image of an engrossing and mysterious natural order is the process at the center of life in these individuals. When the vision comes, the story is "given." But it does not usually stay, or it may tarry at a terrible cost. She may forget loved ones with terrible consequences, she may walk into a busy street in the path of a truck, she may be kidnapped by the fairies. It's terribly painful if it goes and disastrous if it stays. A few can hold on somewhere in the middle but it is hard.

Mary Poppins is not the most typical representative of the work of this group of writers, because of the humor, and yet this book conveys very well the sense of this type of character. We can think of Mary Poppins as being the heroine of the first group turned upside down. On one book jacket, a group of men is eagerly watching her as she drops right out of the blue head first. A depiction of this sort of behavior is characteristic of the creative process of this group of writers—Poppins, like her author, has a splendid upside down manner of presentation. She is all there too; she has her umbrella, all her necessary apparel.

Conflict Between Inner and Outer

In our study, the largest group of women writers showed evidence of conflict between inner and outer realities. They were critical of many aspects of society but also blamed

From *The Rescuers* by Margery Sharp, copyright 1959. Illustration by Garth William. Reprinted by permission of Little, Brown and Company.

From *The Pushcart War* by Jean Merrill, copyright 1964, Young Scott Books. Illustration by Ronni Solbert. Reprinted by permission of Addison-Wesley Publishing Company.

themselves for not living up to social guidelines or to expectations of stern inner voices.

One syndrome in this group recurs repeatedly and deserves special attention. First I'll tell you the sort of story that a woman of this group might write. I am going to use a story by an author who did *not* participate in the study because I want to protect the anonymity of the writers.

An aristocratic mouse named Miss Bianca goes with two humbler male mice to rescue a Norwegian poet imprisoned in the Black Castle. They have dangerous encounters with the warden's giant cat, Mamelouk, but it is with his unwitting aid that they make contact with the poet. Miss Bianca faints, flirts (with the sadistic Mamelouk), writes poems, and is the epitome of the heroine who is as spirited as she is feminine and vice versa. More recently, books of this type have become more serious. The heroines are less archly feminine than Miss Bianca but they still triumph by acts of courage, love, and sacrifice, and the distinctive features of the books remain the struggle with the demonic and the rescue of, or alliance with, a wise or powerful male.

These authors have a typical personal history. The father has been weak or cold or absent. The mother was talented and sometimes altogether admirable. There were few siblings, seldom a brother. This family constellation is often found among male writers, but a male hero in such a case would probably kill a mother dragon with the spiritual aid of a wizard. The hero might sometimes be small and lonely, but he would also be dignified. You can imagine how his story contrasts with that of Miss Bianca and the giant cat.

Perhaps I should go back and explain that by saying that the hero would kill the mother dragon, I don't mean to make an unpleasant remark about the authors' real mothers. I mean that the hero would try to sever his dependence on his mother by developing masculine ways to fulfill his own needs and by identifying with masculine ideals. But a daughter can't do that so well. How is she to get separated from her mother? How is she to obtain and express the "manliness" that her whole family needed and sought through her? And how can she find a mature "feminine" self? This is one of the hard problems in the psychology of contemporary women. The data suggest strongly that women who have had inadequate opportunity to love and rely on a father are the ones for whom an inner male image continues to loom large and ambiguously. The feminine central character is diminished in comparison, and sometimes there is confusion or uncertainty about what the relationship between the heroine and the wise and powerful male is to be. Perhaps the sudden resolutions of some of these books, the slight tendency to woodenness of characters or falsity of feelings may express the author's own residual difficulties in solving these problems of her own past. And that may be why these books are not rated among the very best. On the other hand, many of them have a scope or intensity that grips the reader and captures the imagination. I think that these authors go back to the emotional residues of a significant problem, even if they are somewhat past it as adults. What this type of author writes about, she has also lived. Her work is of great interest to the many father-hungry children and adults in our society and makes an important contribution to children's literature.

Mustering of Inner Reality and Defiance of Society

The psychological process relating "inner" and "outer" realities in a fourth group of women authors can be described as a mustering of inner forces in defiance of society. They have written books about the organization of a disadvantaged group for the purpose of overcoming entrenched evil or conventional stultification. The stories are often humorous. For example, there is one about pushcart peddlers who organize to end the ruthless domination of trucks in a big city. Their main weapon works like a pea-shooter to puncture the inflated tires of the big trucks. Like the previous group, these books emphasize aggression and independence, but in a very different context. The evil is usually not demonic but social: it's right there in the city.

The authors of these stories had the happiest childhoods that I have ever read about in my fifteen years of personality assessment. It makes your heart warm to read about their family life. They had strong and loving parents and usually a good supply of brothers. Their female characters do not take a conventional sex role; their themes suggest the development of an inner strength to cast off traditional authority. One thinks of the civil rights and youth groups of the sixties that had this same formation of peer group against entrenched authority. Studies of protesting youth have often found them to be particularly vigorous, high in ego strength, and advantaged in background, so here is additional similarity. It is interesting that these books antedated the women's movement and may even be said to have anticipated it. And yet, they are not wholly new. In the Edwardian period both men and women wrote books that have a similar structure. A familiar example would be the alignment of Wendy and the Lost Boys against Captain Hook in *Peter Pan*. However, the Edwardian authors seldom convey the sense that the peer group might really win out. The idea that one's efforts may really pay off in the real world makes a lot of difference.

The motive-patterns in these books by women authors can be represented on a graph. The vertical axis represents an heroic dimension that has to do with aggression, achievement and independence. The horizontal axis represents a tender dimension having to do with setting, relationships between characters, tender emotion, and not being very analytical or plot-minded. The first two groups of books that I described are plotted below the mean on the heroic dimension and the second two groups of books score above the mean. After plotting this graph, it becomes obvious that the books of the contemporary sample which emphasize the heroic have been written more recently than the books which score low on this dimension.

The fact that women have increasingly been writing books of the heroic type, whether the Miss Bianca type or the pushcart-war type, seems to me to suggest that creative women are working towards a new identity, one in which there is a new integration of masculine and feminine traits and one which can support the self-image of women as creative in the arts or the world of ideas.

Toward such a conceptualization I would like to offer a model that has developed out of several of these studies of creativity in women. This schema is called "The Creative Woman as a Circle of Friends." I see it as representing a group of companions around a center which is either empty and receptive or contains an emotionally charged mass of ideas which is gradually taking organic shape. The companions represent a cluster of archetypes, if you like, or personality functions or resources. The Owl and the Dwarf are the most conscious, the Serpent Lady and the Bear less so, and John the Baptist is not quite a part of the group at all. He is a picture hanging on the wall or he visits some times but even as a picture he sets standards, concentrates emotion and focuses thought. It is an important aspect of the model that the center is vulnerable. The receptive center is the means by which communication (inner and outer) takes place and impregnation occurs. Presumably the personality functions best when all of the resources are available and can be called upon as needed. The Owl and the Dwarf serve to protect the maiden or the pregnant virgin, and also to shape the creative contents. Without them, the center might be occupied, let us say, by the Housekeeper, whose main concern is to keep the place clean and the doors locked. (In which case John the Baptist would be replaced by the Supreme Court, and burglars would be at the cellar door.)

The Owl is the bird of Athena. It is blind in the day but sees at night, that is, it has inward vision. It often lives close to people but yet apart. It is wise but relatively inarticulate. It feeds on mice, frogs and the like—id material. There is cruelty associated with the Owl, meaning perhaps that it is merciless in its observation or that the introspective attitude suppresses impulses of affection and generosity or devours vitality. After it "digests" the contents of its hunting, like an analytical scholar, the Owl spits up a ball of gray fluff, with neat, clean little bones inside. Creative women have more highly developed owlish attitudes than most people, but it is important to remember that they are not altogether Owls. For one thing, the pregnant Virgin wants to deliver a live birth.

John
the Baptist
(masculine spirit
as guide)

The
Serpent Lady
(Sex, narcissism,
manipulativeness,
charm)

The Bear
(Strength,
maternal protectiveness,
endurance)

The Maiden
(receptive center)
or
The Pregnant Virgin
(developing creative
contents)

The Owl
(Introspectiveness,
observation,
reflection)

The Dwarf
(Ingenuity, craft,
stubbornness,
resistance)

The Creative Woman as a Circle of Friends

Saint John the Baptist Preaching by Auguste Rodin, (detail) bronze, 78¾″ high, 1878. Collection: The Museum of Modern Art, New York. *Snake Goddess (Priestess?),* c. 1600 b.c. (detail) Terracotta, height 13½″. Museum, Candia, Crete. Brown Bear. *The Birth of Venus* by Botticelli, (detail) c. 1480. Uffizi Gallery, France. Snowy Owl. *Sebastian de Morra* by Velasquez, (detail) about 1648. Madrid, Prado.

Similarly, if one thinks of a creative woman's consciousness as having a Dwarf aspect, many relevant ideas are brought together: A love of working with concrete detail, strategies close to earth, knowledge of subterranean passageways and treasures, stubborn resistance to interference, jealous possessiveness, legs too short for trunk and head, a consciousness of shortened stature in the world's eye, a long memory, and so forth. Like the Owl, the Dwarf is not entirely a pleasant fellow. However, in him the creative woman has had her main expression of active aggression. Furthermore, the Dwarf has many good qualities. He is loyal, clever, a hard worker, an excellent craftsman, sometimes irritable but not overbearing.

Dwarves and jesters have both had a rather special relationship to the king. They represent the other side of the king or what the king needs to remember. Although the Dwarf also needs to remember the king, there may be considerable difficulty in actual merger of these "opposites." The creative woman manages relatively well. John the Baptist, at his best, is a figure who signifies the integration of upper and lower. Leonardo da Vinci painted him with one hand pointing up and the other pointing down. He feeds on honey and locusts. He is the Voice crying in the wilderness (creative chaos), "Prepare ye," and he announces the arrival of the divine child. He is the baptizer, by whom the Maiden is immersed into the waters of unconsciousness and raised again into the light. At his weakest he is a "figure-head," cut off from the earthier aspects of the personality and their victim.

Let me describe the other characters more briefly. The Serpent Lady and the Bear, as has been said, do not show so much from the outside. However, the emotional fascination of creative work, the narcissism of the creative person, and a certain seductiveness in the creative product owe much to the Serpent Lady. It is she who sends dreams, jokes, tricks, temptations, warnings, wisdom—if one can read her right. She can bestow bountiful gifts and fearful punishments. Her garments are silver, that is, both black and white. Jung described her eloquently as the Anima. To the creative woman she is perhaps the goddess of the underworld.

The Bear is a massive force, life-giving, protecting, though its hug can crush, and sometimes it eats its young. It is little conscious of itself. The single-minded, silent endurance which the creative woman may undergo while her work is developing reflects the contribution of the Bear. The weight of the Bear enables her to bear down, to suffer child-bearing.

The Maiden is always succumbing to influence, rather as the White Knight was always falling off his horse. She has big, vacant eyes which long for unconsciousness. It makes one feel somewhat dizzy to look into them, but she is the spirit of responsiveness, appreciation, worship and awe.

The Pregnant Virgin feels the embryo taking shape. She gives it her life blood unconsciously and unambivalently. Heedless of the outside world, she feels the joy and wonder of her garden.

Many fairy stories may be interpreted in terms of these various components. "Rumpelstiltskin" is the story of an episode during which the Dwarf did so much work and became so important that he threatened to make off with the baby. "Snow White and the Seven Dwarves" tells how the Maiden fled from the Evil Queen, a negative version of the Serpent Lady. She becomes Housekeeper for some dwarves. The Dwarf is multiplied here, as is so often the case, when the resource represented is not well-developed or is insufficient. When the dwarves are away, Snow White succumbs to the Queen's temptations. She sinks into unconsciousness, from which only the Prince, another aspect of the masculine principle, can save her.

Many women who engage or want to engage in creative activity are made anxious by fear of their vulnerability (femininity) or their destructive and phallic impulses (masculinity). In this schema I am trying to illustrate what we may mean by the bisexuality or androgny of a creative person and that it need not be frightening. It is the patterning and awareness of these components that is important.

Some years ago Phyllis Greenacre suggested that gifted women often identify their talent as phallic and then, ashamed at having it, try to hide it or deny it. Or, along the lines pointed out by Esther Harding, they overcompensate. Today many women need the sense that their creativity can be solidly based on their own body. The schema is helpful in this respect and it also suggests the variety and vitality of personality resources that are available to women *now*—not merely to be dreamed of in some future society.

Some wits have suggested that the mystery of woman is an empty hole. The void, yes, but also the sea is the inner reality of women. And since the drought of the body arrives in its time, I would like to close with a glimpse of inner reality from the writings of an elderly creative woman.

In the midst of a depression following a divorce, one of the women authors of fantasy in our study came into possession of a remarkable house, which was built during the Crusades and which has figured prominently in most of her work. She is a very old woman now—in her eighties—and she has lived out an analogy between that house and the full depths of her psyche. In one of her books she has the elderly woman tenant of this house say, "Sitting here alone for the longest series of wordless winter nights, I feel neither shut in nor shut off, but rather like the heart inside living ribs" and elsewhere she says, "I believe that if my house were magnified as big as the sea it would show as much sparkle, as much rhythm and vitality, as much passion as the sea." □

Sister Helena Steffens-Meier. Photo by Linda Rich.

DEVELOPING CREATIVITY

Discussion Leader: Agnes Denes
Artist and lecturer.

Agnes Denes: What interests me most is developing in women a new expression. I'm not saying that women have not been innovative, they have. But there is a tendency to imitate man, to tread on safe ground because we haven't had role models as women. I wish women would now dare to try new innovative fields, wherever that field is—don't look back, don't look to anybody else who has done it before and don't be afraid of criticism. I truly believe that in the face of innovation, discrimination will diminish.

Creativity is a very personal, private thing. Nobody can develop it for you. The road cannot be made easier to walk on, the question can't be answered, the only thing that can happen is that one learns how to ask the question.

Elvie Moore: We are just a small segment of the potential creative women in our society. There would be far more women if we had reinforcement and if we had assistance. I think creativity has too long remained an upper middle-class phenomenon mainly because of finances. When you have burdens forced upon you by a male-dominated society, you are always in a conflict state. There has to be not only psychological but economic reinforcement to help women to break through. When we start testing these questions, we are going to start talking about new values. The family structure, for instance, has worked to the detriment of most women. You cannot relate unless you have support, and you cannot have support unless you have a viable situation. I find myself in great despair at times when I cannot write and when I look at my situation I realize that it's because of many real impediments that I cannot write. Possibly things would be better if I were in a communal situation and my day to work was Tuesday and the rest of the week I could

devote myself to being creative. Our role is not just psychological, it is also sociological and we have to deal with that.

Valentina Litvinoff: If an artist is only preoccupied with the details and the minutiae of her work—with the hard sweat—or the curator with her museum, we're not allowing for the larger inspirations of the current social scene. How these changes relate to us haven't been explored. What are the groups or the issues which are compelling change in our culture today? Let's say the third world, the struggle for peace, the struggle of black liberation—all of these are part and parcel of the women's question because the very same forces that are keeping us in a state of subjugation and discrimination are also perpetuating other problems. We're not going to get very far if we see our problem as one issue or one group of issues; but if we see them as interrelated and part of the whole social scene, then we're going to be able to get larger inspirations and larger perspectives for our art.

If I as an artist have a very narrow world of paint, of manipulation of my craft, well and good, that's my craft. Or if I want to compete with current trends, current fashion or whatever, and make my work shocking, I should be entitled to do it, but do we want to spend the consciousness which we have raised to just follow trends? If we identify ourselves with the forces of today and change ourselves as human beings, it will affect the very fiber of our art.

Agnes Denes: I agree that society and change in the world has an awful lot to do with creativity and ourselves as women. There used to be a time when not only woman but any creative person had to go into a hole in the wall and create. I don't think we can do that any longer and that's why I gave up painting. Painting was putting color on color, changing shapes and form,

Elvie Moore at Women and the Arts Conference. Photos by Bob Black. Courtesy: The Johnson Foundation.

and there were issues outside that were more important to me.

Lee Weiss: One of the ways we can develop creativity in women is to develop markets for it, to develop the awareness that women are capable of creating.

Marjorie Kreilick: What about the role models of women in history? I really disagree with you about art being involved with social change.

Elizabeth Janeway: Can an historian speak for just a minute? If you think of the outburst of creativity in the Renaissance or narrow it down and take Elizabethan England, you have an example of social change producing a great outburst of creativity. You had first of all the weakening of the role of the church which had been very powerful for art in its time but had become a stranglehold. And with the discovery of America and the idea of a New World and the inflow of gold and precious metals to Europe, the economic base of the society was increased. There was economic rise and a great increase in trade and all of these things combined brought forth the outburst of creativity we recognize in the sixteenth century.

Elvie Moore: It would seem to me that the creative process involves being receptive to new values. How do you know what is new unless you yourself are going through the process? Maybe we have to go through pain, maybe we have to test the values by doing something which we ourselves may not want to do. Maybe we have to become real mavericks and thrust ourselves into a new world. And we should not necessarily be so presumptuous as to put the label of creativity on this process because it is also the process of being. You are in effect going into a void and you are not afraid of it because you are in a process and you are freeing yourself of the logic of being mechanized by a society that demands control of your actions in order for you to be professional. When we speak of the professional, we are labeling a process that we have no right to label. How can we do this if we are to put forth new values? We may have to go into very unfamiliar realms and we may be chastised and cast out by Western society for it.

ON CREATIVITY *

the universe was created without human touch then humanity was created there is a Creator
the Maker as god or nature which is creative or humanity which is creative within nature
which has created it
    and so humanity evolved and went on creating itself.
what is creativity?
     a beginning causation production imagination originality

                     oh yes, that!
         creativity seeks its own level

what is there for a human
to create but to try and
      transcend,
his finite existence
and search the mysteries
of life- his life- the-
universe- himself- all-
of- it-
creativity is invention, unique invention, divine function, neologism

a new idea, a rationale-intermediate between life and death - the abstract, the thought, the
absolute

what is creative?
arranging flowers in a vase, inhaling the morning mist and knowing it's life, building an em-
pire and through it power, societal power, surviving in a slum, meditation, transcendence,
the searching intellect, truth!

     (the power to create)(is not the same)(as creative power)

    the mind possessing universal validity - art revealing a universal
       truth - reaching for that truth!
             to what end?
      good
questions are good questions are better questions are a way of life
         better

what is creativity?
a forever rising knowledge and deepening awareness emerging from the long winding tip
of a flowing plant or the roots of a tree

what is creativity?

  the
    visualization
       of
        the
         mechanism
           of
            the
             workings
               of
                hypotheses

---

*A few weeks after the conference took place Agnes Denes sent us the following impressions
on creativity.

analyses
>   the
>   quest
>   the
>   probe
>   seeking
>   naming
the search   searching   searching   searching   searching   goddammit

immortality in more than human terms
overcoming the finiteness   beauty

'the correspondence of the mind with the object of its knowledge'

creating creatively is fun but creating the ultimate is immortality

where does creativity come from?

Lost Dreams by Joanne Leonard (Berkeley, Cal.), 1971.

love!
hunger!

hunger for wanting and knowing and doing—opening the door to my studio and seeing a new idea unfold half born but alive—defining and redefining testing the strength of the new-born—nurturing it

it comes from dark into light
from wanting to change things
from nothing to something

it comes from tree tops and handshakes and smiles and river bottoms. its in the rushing water and the rocks. its in the eye of the beholder. its in my bedroom three in the morning

the urge is a whip in a merciless hand it whips till the deed is done, done to perfection for there is no other way. and the finite existence becomes not external living but living the way living is one with a silent universe turbulent with hidden creativity

true artistry begins by creating on new levels where what you create has never existed before.

do I mean true and complete innovation?
like discovering radium?
having a half-life of 1620 years and
emitting alpha particles and gamma rays

yes and no

radium had always been there
it had to be separated refined defined

I create from other art before me. yet there has never been any art like mine before me. my art is before me. that's enough.

life is in the way of art   but art is in spite of life.

is art a priori?
is art intentional?

I must change everything I come in contact with. I must pull the lid off and peek inside then show everyone else what I've seen I must cut away and unfold reveal and dig into mix up and rearrange reevalue and transplant. I am a messy creator but show me one who is neat look

what a mess He made!
and isn't it great?

IMAGERY IN COMMUNICATION MEDIA

Discussion Leader: Perry Miller Adato
Producer and director, WNET Channel 13,
New York.

Perry Miller Adato: What we're talking about falls into two general areas. First, what is the imagery of women in the media and how can it be changed? Second, what is the status of the woman artist or woman worker in the media and how can it be changed?

The second, of course, relates directly to the first because through it the imagery can be changed. If you get women who become producers, directors, and managers and who are in control, you will have a great deal of change in what is seen.

Television generally breaks down into dramatic programming, daytime and nighttime, commercials, children's programs and news—news breaks down into talk shows and documentaries and peripheral kinds of programs. We all know the stereotypes of the dramatic series—the woman as sex object, the virginal good girl, the earth-mother figure, the menace, the woman who's inept at dealing with technology, etc. In a study a woman writer did on all the dramatic daytime serials something like ninety-four percent of the programs had a woman who was planning to have a baby, a woman who was unhappy because she couldn't have a baby, a woman who was keeping her marriage together because she was planning on having a baby—the emphasis on maternity is not to be believed.

In the commercials you see the bungling woman, the woman needing the strong authority figure, the woman who doesn't know what to do and the announcer, of course, is the male who will tell her how she can solve her problems by using a certain product. One interesting example is how the actress who was to play a dumb wife who was making terrible coffee refused to do it and she suggested right on the spot how that Max-Pax commercial could be rewritten and they let her do it. This is a very good illustration of how very easily a positive image can be projected at the same time that you sell the product. She now says, "If you're like me and have a lot of

Joni Mitchell. Courtesy: Lookout Management.

important things to do and don't want to have to spend your time worrying about your coffee, use Max-Pax. It's always right."

I was at a very interesting conference at Cornell with a lot of women filmmakers and in almost every case they admitted that the first time that they were able to make a film was through the help and encouragement of a man who said you can do it and practically pushed them into it. After, of course, once they had done it, it was possible for them to go on. My first film was on Dylan Thomas *(The World I Grieve)* and the only reason I directed that was because I was a producer and there was no one else around to do it, and my boss said, "You can do it; you just go in there and tell everybody that you're the boss." But it's very hard to be the boss, and this is part of what I call the internal problem. We're very afraid of being authoritative, we're afraid of telling people what to do because we don't want people to say she's unfeminine, she's a bitch. I found that I was, I still am, very intimidated by the mystique of the camera and by the male cameraman and I've spoken about it to men and men are not intimidated.

There was a major proposal which came from Dallas and it has now been funded by the Corporation for Public Broadcasting. A New York (man) producer thought that it would be nice to do a program with *MS* since the magazine has been so enormously successful. Now, why hadn't a woman come up with that program?

Faith Ringgold: But are you assuming that he got the idea? He might have gotten the idea from several women.

Perry Miller Adato: But, that's not the point. Why did he have the guts?

Kay Clarenbach: But don't you think that several women might have already tried to do that? I know groups of women who have gone to all kinds of places with television proposals—maybe not the right places.

Perry Miller Adato: I also have a proposal for a similar program on the status of women. They didn't take my idea though

and so I gave up. I should have been smart enough to think that if I had *MS* magazine behind me, they would have been forced to do it.

It is encouraging to all of us, however, that behind the words of angry feminism, there is action. Two years ago Women for Equality in the Media, a group headed by director Francine Parker, marched on the American film industry charging overt discrimination and demanding that a representative fifty-two percent women be admitted to programs which are partially funded by the National Endowment of the Arts. We didn't get what we wanted, but more women have been admitted. Soon after Kathleen Nolan of the Screen Actors Guild organized a women's committee. They met alone and then, in conjunction with S.A.G.'s minorities committee, they went to network studios, writers and casting directors and they came prepared with statistics, ideas and solutions and answers.

At the same time Diana Gould organized a group of thirty women in the Writer's Guild of America. Until this group formed women thought that they had to have a low profile to succeed. Now that they have a committee it is a way for women to communicate. The S.A.G. and W.G.A. women's committees worked together to produce a thirty-minute tape program, "Women Speak," which shows that yesterday's feminists were voicing the same problems of women artists today.

Within the television and motion picture studios a group of secretaries met to protest the concentration of women in low-paying, dead-end positions. Last February forty women and men, carrying picket signs and chanting, "Dino's a real dingaling," marched from a Buena Vista park to NBC studios in Burbank protesting the sexist stereotypes on the Dean Martin show and the Golddiggers, both produced by Greg Harrison. The protest plus other complaints caused the Dingaling Sisters to be dropped.

In April two thousand people met at UCLA to hear sixty industry women speak out on sexism in the media. The size and enthusiasm of the audience indicated to the organizer a widening of community support. In May the publisher of the *Hollywood*

Reporter brought together established women to form "Women in Film," a national clearinghouse for jobs and an information center. The group grew from twelve to seventy-five members, all listed in the recently published directory *Women in Film.* The women have been using the directory, putting together deals, helping each other, and not waiting around for the studios to come to them. In November Cine-Women was formed. Our main thrust, says the executive director, is the establishment of a women's film center in Los Angeles coupled with the intent to work with other organizations for the drastic revisions needed in both the image and the status of women in film.

The Los Angeles National Organization for Women has offered its support to groups in pressuring networks, studios, and unions. The National Feminist Party met with studio representatives and network representatives to apply pressure in the areas of hiring and image. Two feminist film publications are in various stages of development. Women are forming production companies and one company has already gone into production. Creative Women of America is acting as an umbrella group and an information clearinghouse for more than two hundred groups worldwide.

Television stations and networks are extremely sensitive to public pressure. You would be astounded at how sensitive they are to public pressure; twenty letters can get people all upset, one hundred letters could cause major change, and a thousand letters could cause a revolution. If women only realized that one thousand letters to one station could result in a series of films about women. I would absolutely guarantee that if Channel 13 got one thousand letters tomorrow we would have a women's film festival that I have tried to get on for ages.

I have a quote worth listening to: "The artist is always the dew line for change, he sees ahead and projects the new images before most of us are aware that the present ones are outmoded." So the excuse that images and movies project women as they are is not good enough. They must also show women as they could be. When blacks insisted that network drama and commercials begin to project positive images of blacks and give blacks behavior models that young and old could identify with, the networks balked because they felt that this would not be an honest depiction of society. After all, they said, how many black doctors are there, how many heads of companies are blacks; black women play maids because maids are black, black men play truck drivers because truck drivers are black. Sure, the black movement said, black doctors may be the exception but until you show him on television he'll keep on being the exception. So directly as a result of the new power of the black movement and the black audience, television shows were suddenly peopled with new black images— black doctors, black mayors, black teachers, black detectives, black heroes, black heroines—and commercials suddenly were full of black people. Now this doesn't mean that the black battle has been won. This is just to point out how quickly in the last few years a change has been made.

Now, when the money crunch came at NET, a lot of programs were eliminated and two programs catering to black audiences (*Black Journal* and *Soul*) were cancelled or scheduled to be cancelled. There was so much protest and they were so well organized that there was no choice, *Black Journal* and *Soul* went back on and the same thing happened this year when we're poorer than ever. There are not going to be as many *Black Journals* and *Soul,* but we cannot eliminate them because there is too much organized support. If I seem to be talking very frequently about the experience of the black movement, it's because the women's movement has to learn from the black movement. I think that our condition is similar and our solutions lie in the same directions.

Faith Ringgold: I am frustrated from listening and looking at television and radio and only seeing male images. I am really very fed up with it. I look at *Black Journal* and I see men sitting around talking to men and on other black programs I see black men talking to black men or white men. I remember when there were very few or no black people on television. When a black person was on television, we used to get on the phone (we had a circuit of calls) and we'd call and say, get Channel 3 quick because there's a black person on. Sometimes I used to take my dial and turn the light down so that everybody looked black. Well, *now* I have the problem of looking only at men and I have had it. Personally I don't care whether *Black Journal* is on the air or not because it is still not including more than half of the population of black people who are women. I am sure there are other black women like me who want to see black women. Even in the flashes of black people in films on black youth or a film like *Wattstax,* they depict black men only. I know that we're really on the low end of the pole but we do exist. I want to be one black woman who makes it quite clear that it's not enough to see black men on the media, I want to see black women.

Perry Miller Adato: What have you done specifically? What do you think can be done to get more women on?

Faith Ringgold: Well, I think that women have to speak up. I think generally women do like to see male images, black women, white women, all women, they like to look at a man. Why is this? It doesn't make any difference what the guy looks like, if he's saying anything sensible or not, or whether he has any talent or ability or anything to offer. It just must be male images. Women have to deal with why this is so.

Doris Freedman: I'm a little concerned that we're not talking more about the process of action. What about the economics? The most insipid thing is to see the black woman in commercials in that same stupid role that the white woman has played. And this goes back to who is paying for what. What are we doing to change that absolutely degrading image of all women regardless of color? Our power there is the economic power which is what the commercial is catering to.

Perry Miller Adato: Look what happened when we started boycotting meat. Immediately the meat boycott had the whole country in an uproar. If we would organize a boycott in connection with those television commercials, they would change overnight.

Clare Spark-Loeb: I think it helps to talk about two categories of media: commercial media and listener-sponsored. Because the economic conditions, the kinds of freedom and the contexts are totally different. It's ridiculous to have a feminist film followed by sexist commercials. It nullifies the content of the program. Second, not just any woman will do. The question has always been: we've got to get a woman on the panel. As far as I'm concerned, a woman who is not connected with a flourishing feminist movement in which decisions and strategy and tactics are thought out collectively as part of an overall strategy will not have any great effect on making social change. I cannot be emphatic enough about this. And I think it will only happen on community-controlled media whether it's cable television or listener-sponsored radio or educational television.

I would like to talk right now about something that's happening in Los Angeles; an action which all the women's groups are united in fighting. It's a good case study of how the women's movement is exploited to pay male directors and to feed the voyeuristic habits of our society. A man who has done a play with narcotics addicts in New York came to the head of a theatre group and said that he wanted to do something with women. He would advertise for women in the community who had been "shitted upon" by the society, and get them together to do tapes. He did not want any women who had anything to do with any kind of consciousness-raising or any alliance with the feminist movement, and he would prove that you could make a play out of women baring their souls about their lives. And he is doing that and it is being produced. I was privileged, I was told, to be allowed to see a rehearsal. He is getting a large salary; the woman playwright who put the tapes together is being paid very little, and the women players are being paid almost nothing at all. Their state of political consciousness is almost nowhere. It sounds like the darkies are just stretching and yawning on the plantation and noticing that something is wrong. The play is called *L.A. Woman.* It will not only be produced at the Mark Taper Forum but it will be on NET and this is within a context when no feminist material can get on our television stations.

Perry Miller Adato: I do not agree, unfortunately, that the only way that images will change is through community channels and video tape. I think that they are extremely important and that everybody has to become very sophisticated about the channel situation and the possibilities for video tape, but the number of people who will be reached by that is very small. We have to use pressure at the same time—getting other people to write letters, the chain letter idea, for example.

Kay Clarenbach: Well, I think I'm going to be dead and buried before we get enough changes if I've got to write five letters to five people.

Perry Miller Adato: But that is one step. That's how we got Women's Strike for Peace started—by having every women who was at a particular demonstration bring ten women the next time. Every technique is a small one but everything has to be done.

Faith Ringgold: I believe in the power of the dial, you turn it off. I try to remember what products are sponsoring the programs which are ignoring my image and I just don't buy them because they have sponsored a certain show. We haven't done it that much but I think that's power. When the sponsors know that certain women are not buying their products because they are producing programs which are demeaning to women, maybe they will change.

Perry Miller Adato: I think this is very important but you have to let the sponsor know through letters, through organized action.

Wilma Ringstrom: Unfortunately, the case of the woman and the case of the feminist are two entirely different approaches and different thoughts and ideas right now but I don't think that one necessarily precludes the other. I'm speaking to the feminists right now: there may be some of us who are never going to be part and parcel and wholly sisters with you while at the same time we have a respect for your ideas and where you are. It might not be totally empathic but it is nevertheless cooperative. There will be other forces and they will be part of the whole scene.

Kay Clarenbach: I was just reminded of what happened at the *Ladies Home Journal.* If you want some fun reading, there is a

testimonial by John Mack Carter in the Congressional Hearings on the Equal Rights Amendment back in 1970 on what happened the day that the women from the *Ladies Home Journal,* joined by other women, dropped in unannounced and gave him the most instructive eleven hours of his life and converted him. A lot of us hadn't been buying the *Ladies Home Journal,* and it really didn't drive them out of business, and it didn't really affect their policies; but they are now making real efforts as a result of that action.

I know groups of women and feminists who are actually going in to sponsors and advertisers and advertising firms and saying, "Now, look, this is the way you can do it; this is the reason why we are offended by what you're doing now." If they don't understand why it is offensive, they explain it in kindergarten language and get some specific changes. I'm in favor of all kinds of action, whether it's consumer action or direct confrontation.

Clare Spark-Loeb: Can I just add another clarification? I wouldn't have called myself a feminist a year and a half ago; I always said they instead of we, but I've never put down another woman for anything. We're all at a different place and I hope that nobody is put off because I appear to be more radical, more activist and more ready to do things than someone else. But I do think, just like a scientist, that the kinds of problems we choose to attack and the way that we do it reflects our larger view of society and long-range goals. I think we need to talk to each other more and I hate to see people in media divide women from each other in the way that has been done. We really haven't talked about that—where within the context of interviews or panels women are used to pick each other apart. It's a very destructive thing to do.

Perry Miller Adato: I think the important thing, and the thing that all of us can agree on, unfortunately, is that the consciousness of the general audience has to be changed. If we could change the abortion bill and get positive abortion bills passed, I think anything can be done. Let's end on that positive note. We've simply got to go back and raise the consciousness of the audience and take the power in our own hands. □

Alice B. Toklas and Gertrude Stein from *When This You See, Remember Me,*
film by Perry Miller Adato (New York).

MAKING CULTURAL INSTITUTIONS MORE RESPONSIVE TO SOCIAL NEEDS

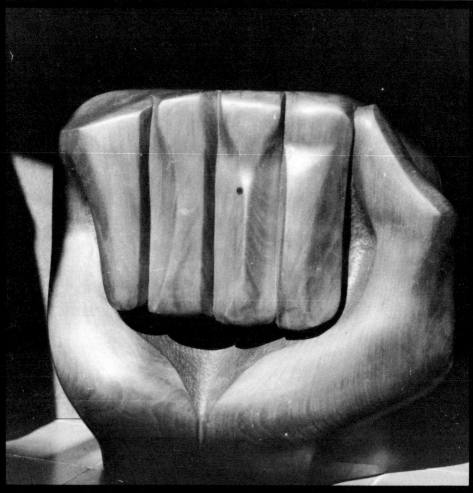

Unity by Elizabeth Catlett (Mexico).

by Grace Glueck
Arts Correspondent and Assistant
Metropolitan Editor, The New York Times.

When the topic of "Making Cultural Institutions More Responsive to Social Needs" was first broached to me, my reaction was so negative that I had to sniff all around it. Do I really believe that cultural institutions; that is, if we define a cultural institution as one that preserves, nurtures, fosters, and disseminates artistic expression, can be responsive to social needs? What are *social needs* anyway? Since a work of art is the product of an individual mind and by its very nature a comment rather than an action, how effective an instrument of social change can we expect it to be? Aren't we indulging in the fascist fantasies of Nazi Germany and Russia if we expect cultural institutions to exert social force? Pushing these rather downbeat thoughts around in my head, I decided finally and fortunately for my talk that, yes, there is a social need that institutions must respond to and that is the need to heighten our awareness of our own humanity. After all, culture reflects the better side of us—the side that feels, thinks, has a world view as opposed to the side that acts out of expedience, greed, and bodily necessity. To the degree that we experience our common humanity, I guess we become better political animals. So, in this way, cultural institutions do respond to social needs. They do not affect society directly and politically, but they may help us to change our view of ourselves, or our vision, if you will. And by exhibiting the work of all of us with talent, men, women, blacks, whites, whatever, they can help destroy the damaging cultural stereotypes that we cherish about each other.

So far, so good—in theory. But we know that most cultural institutions are quite inflexible, that while they may be good at displaying objects or performances, they do not reach far enough into our lives. Surely there are ways of getting to more of us better—giving not only the artist more chance for contact with his audience, actual and potential, but also giving the audience a chance at a more flexible response than simply watching. I have no radical proposals as to how to bring this about; that is, how to help an individual become more aware of himself as an embodiment of his culture so that he can see himself and his roots as a part of our general humanity. We all know some tentative innovations that are being tried with varying degrees of success by institutions that consider themselves progressive. Tom Hoving's disastrous show at the Metropolitan Museum a couple of years ago,

"Harlem On My Mind," was one example of a patronizing exhibition put on by an upper class white institution. Although, as someone later remarked, think of the hullabaloo Hoving saved himself by not putting on a show called "Women On My Mind." But there have been better attempts—the Walker Art Center in Minneapolis, for example, has developed a program of taking the museum to the public, providing art classes for children, for instance, held in such offbeat locations as TV stations, parks, and planning offices. The Brooklyn Children's Museum on the fringes of the black ghetto has developed MUSE, an innovative mini-museum where kids can play with animals, borrow costumes, and study such subjects as painting, jazz, or even piloting airplanes. The staid Smithsonian in Washington sponsors Anacostia, a museum in a black neighborhood that stages such realistic exhibitions as, say, a show on rats. And the Metropolitan Museum itself has started a collection of so-called primitive art, bestowing on that art a cachet and a status that is particularly meaningful to the disenfranchised people who are its heirs. If, along with blacks, white kids learn that African art is a strong and powerful expression as meaningful as Western art, that could help to change the white child's concept of the African heritage.

Pressure tactics have also been tried with institutions that do not move toward greater social responsiveness. I am sure a lot of you will remember that, at the Whitney Museum in New York a couple of years ago, a group of women artists succeeded by demonstrations and protests in getting the museum to up the quota of women in its annual exhibition from between five and a half and ten per cent to twenty-two per cent. The Whitney also put on an exhibition of the work of black artists after considerable pressure and so did the Boston Museum. To the horror of my elitest friends and colleagues who say, "But does this kind of thing encourage quality," I respond that I believe in such pressure. I don't know that shows of work by women or by blacks or other artists as groups are particularly meaningful as a statement, but if such shows give museums the impetus to go out and look for talent among groups that they have hitherto ignored, if it leads them to search out women artists or to go into Harlem and elsewhere to find talented people and opens institutional resources to them, then yes, such pressure certainly has its use.

If there is still a question in anyone's mind, by the way, about the ignoring of women artists by major museums, I'll cite some statistics from a story I covered that seem fairly representative. In April, 1972, "Women in the Arts," which characterized itself as the largest group in New York City concerned with ending discrimination against women artists, came out for an exhibition called "Women Choose Women" to be selected by its own membership. They demonstrated in front of various museums, particularly The Museum of Modern Art. Among other complaints, the group charged that out of one thousand one-artist shows in its forty-three years, the museum had presented only five by women; that in ten leading New York galleries, 94.6—I know that sounds sort of Ivory Soapish—but 94.6 per cent of the artists represented were men. A MOMA employee stationed at the Museum's entrance passed out a hastily prepared rebuttal that said the museum was really nice to women artists— it had actually only staged two hundred ninety-three one-artist shows since 1929, its beginning, and of those, twenty-seven or approximately nine per cent were devoted to women artists. The rebuttal also asserted that in the painting and sculpture department ninety-three of the one thousand eighty artists represented were women or slightly less than ten per cent—which brought the comment from one of the participants, "That's a rebuttal?"

Sure, women want big museum shows and big critics to write about them. While deploring the chauvinism of white males, women and blacks want their attention as confirmation of status. But I'd like to suggest here that even while searching for this kind of recognition, they can make cultural institutions—the existing cultural institutions—more socially responsive by setting out to explore their own values through alternative institutions. A friend of mine, a writer, recently lamented the decline of little magazines as places for writers "to be bad in." I knew what she meant. She wanted a place where writers could be themselves, develop an identity, let down their hair in a

Portail de la Mort by Niki de Saint Phalle, assemblage, 1963. Courtesy: Alexander Iolas Gallery, New York City and Paris.

supportive context of sympathetic colleagues. Institutions should be developed—and they are being developed—and run by women that are not on the order of the great cultural agencies but that give women a chance to study and work in terms of their own identities. They should be able to do this without a censoring male or sophisticated audience watching in judgment. I don't say that women should seek these groups out exclusively as places of exposure; one ultimately needs the tough judgment of the world outside. But such organizations do already exist—The Feminist Art Program at the California Institute of the Arts, for example, which works to help students find themselves as women and as artists; a Women's Art Center in New York devoted exclusively to women has dance classes, a filmmakers group, and facilities to show paintings; the Women's History Research Center in Berkeley has developed art history courses that study women's role in Western art and raises questions about specifically feminine imagery. Such preoccupations may not be of immediate interest to a male or to a mixed audience but this questioning process, this need for "a place to be bad in," is important for women who are seeking full identities. They can profit from study and exhibition in a protective environment of an alternative institution. But, more importantly, alternative institutions can challenge the staid assumptions of more established organizations. Idealistic, iconoclastic, more in touch with less establishment constituencies, they can affect the thinking of larger institutions such as—to use a glib comparison—the *Village Voice* has influenced *The New York Times*.

But we have been talking so far about affecting institutions from without, the attempt on the part of women and other groups to try and change their external presentations. The real change, of course, can't come about until these institutions are hit from within, that is, in terms of their trustees, their administration, and their employees, the people who work for them. My definition of a cultural institution, I should say at this point, is fairly flexible. Because I know most about museums, I have been talking in terms of them, but a cultural institution could also be, of course, a ballet company, a symphony orchestra,

even the institution for which I work, *The New York Times,* insofar as it serves as a molder of cultural opinion. And here I would like to make a distinction between non-profit cultural institutions—which most are—and profit-making ones. For our purposes, the differences are very important. Non-profit cultural institutions are inherently different from profit-making ones in that the former tend to be governed by moneyed boards of trustees who are also involved with corporations—but who are less venturesome in their institutional commitments than in their corporate outlook. They do a lot less for the employees of the museums they run than they do for those in their corporations. Far from being explorative, daring, or avant garde in their concepts, most non-profit cultural institutions are reluctant to get involved in anything that will risk the disfavor of their trustees. On the other hand, when they operate as businessmen, the trustees are likely to latch on to a trend, whatever their personal feelings, if there is money in it. When TV network officials sensed there was a market of black people out there, they began to incorporate blacks in their advertisements. The possibility of social change developing through culture-oriented or should I say culture-manipulating corporations is thus more realistic than through non-profit making institutions. Non-profit trustees are generally not responsive to the needs of their own institutional employees, both men and women, much less to the community at large. Trustees of museums, for example, pay professional staffs at a far lower rate than the people they employ in their corporations—on the theory, presumably, that in a contest between prestige and earnings, employees of non-profit institutions should share in the non-profit. While accepting unions in their own corporations, trustees fight against professional staff associations—milder versions of unions or guilds—which are allowed to come into being only after debilitating compromise. But what non-profit trustees and management are susceptible to is pressure and publicity. Women at the Metropolitan Museum of Art last year, for example, went to the Attorney General's office to initiate an investigation into why they were paid less and given lesser jobs than men with the same background and experience. The Met signed an assurance of discontinuance—a very gentlemanly legal ploy whereby the sued party agrees to stop a practice it does not admit to ever having practiced. At this point, women at the Met are hopefully on their way up from the job ghetto to which the museum had consigned them. And it was partly because of pressure from the budding staff association, mostly composed of women, at the Museum of Modern Art that the museum voluntarily began to contribute to the New York State unemployment compensation program in October, 1970. In New York, the Metropolitan, the Whitney, the Guggenheim, and even Governor Rockefeller's pet project, the Museum of Primitive Art, did not join the benefit program until January, 1971, when compliance was made mandatory by law.

Let's face it, however, the number of women in top administrative positions in cultural agencies is dismally low. Again a statistic or two by way of example—of seven hundred fifty colleges surveyed in 1970 by the College Art Association, for example, only five per cent had women as chairwomen of their Fine Arts Departments; of seventy-odd big museum members of the Association of Art Museum Directors which takes in museums with budgets of over $100,000, only two are women. Museums, of course, *employ* women—there are large numbers with the rank of curator, but they rarely have wide decision-making powers. There are also lots of women members of boards of trustees, chosen mostly for their money and social clout. But generally they tend to let the men on the board make their decisions for them. And there are many women volunteers who are sometimes (when they have money) lured into make-work projects which necessitate frequent teas and dinner parties.

Museums have, in fact, consistently employed more women than men, but that's because they come cheaper. In the recent past, say, at the Museum of Modern Art, genteel young women who were not dependent on salaries found a pleasant place to work and identification with a posh board of trustees. They were paid even less than the men, because they were women, and they made few demands, for the very same reason.

But the faithful retainer mentality is now being rejected by a different sort of woman, often highly skilled, socially concerned,

and ready to fight. For example, the Modern's woman-dominated staff association struck the museum last October in an attempt to win participation in policy-making decisions on the part of the trustees and the administration.

A woman's point of view can make a vital difference to an institution, as I know from my own experience at *The New York Times*. In our insistence that cultural institutions hire more women for responsible jobs, we must ask that they be women who are fully conscious of their identity as women, who are as unambiguous as possible about their feelings as women, those who are not simply brainwashed editions of men (you see too many of those). While using our intellectual passion and our convictions, we should not be ashamed also to exercise those faculties in us that, possibly, because of our long disenfranchisement, have made us different from men. I expect to get an argument here but I'll indulge in some sweeping generalities— I think we, as executives, have greater insight into the way that people relate to one another. We have less warlike, aggressive patterns of thought. We are not less competitive, but I think our idea of winning is more complex. I think also we are freer to expose ourselves, more willing to show a certain humanity. Because we have less to protect, that is, we are quicker to drop the prerogative of status when we are called on to give a personal response. We are likely to be more sensitive to questions of morale. Also, since the codes and conventions of professional behavior are masculine, we are less likely, it seems to me, to be afraid of the unconventional. As professionals, women, I have noticed tend to be less formal and more approachable than men. Most of us don't play little power games or indulge in the small power strategies. We are perhaps more willing to listen. Men could use some of the informality and honesty that I find in women executives that I work with. Men have to appear to be very firm and decisive, controlled, and authoritative, whereas if they could learn to reveal their hesitations and uncertainties, they would be better able to deal with people and win their loyalty.

On the negative side, women have not been conditioned to take responsibility. They tend to duck it, to be less bold, less willing to take a gamble. Men say that about us and it's true. We are not so good at making the big decisions and we are terribly afraid of affront. As women executives we have a special opportunity to work for women and for the liberation of the institutions that hire us. And they are hiring us more and more. But to do this most effectively, we must simply reject the prejudices of our peers, publicly and explicitly. We will find that our own positions are enhanced if we behave like women and we must not repudiate our membership in a so-called subordinate group. Let it all hang out. The baggage we bring as women to cultural institutions may bring a touch more humanity to them. □

RESPONSE

Grace Glueck: What is social responsiveness on the part of the cultural institution?

Patricia Burnett: I would certainly like to see museums put on more shows for women and the only way they are going to do that is if we unite and put strong pressure on them. I think we should get to the women trustees in the museums and the women who are running the galleries, and raise their consciousness so that they will not feel alienated from the issue. And my last suggestion is that we have more women jurors.

Grace Glueck: When I suggested to the director of the Museum of Modern Art that they have a women's show (a concept that I think would shock the Modern out of existence), he looked at me as though I had suddenly questioned the sanctity of the Virgin Mary. He said, "We couldn't possibly allow one group to dominate the museum." I do believe that a museum should have a women's show but I question again whether women's shows as such have a statement to make about women as women. As I said before the value of such shows lie in the fact that museums must search out the talent to put on those shows and thus give women some exposure. If that's the reason for putting on those shows, yes, I'm all for it. But I also feel that women should be shown more in context with men and with other artists. I think we should insist on it. If you have too many

women's shows it becomes a kind of talking to each other, a talking to oneself.

Linda Nochlin: How is it that museum directors are always happy to have national shows? For example, they are always happy to have shows related to a historical period or a stylistic movement, but not sex discriminated shows. It is a very interesting point. What, for example, is the mystique behind American Abstract Art? This was a great movement, which had a mystique, and consisted of a group of American artists, of whom a lot were really different but happened to be friends who communicated and shared common goals. That was considered an all right thing— although, from a certain point of view, you might call it dirty nationalism. Why is it that a women's show or a black show is not considered in the same way? It is considered instead a sort of perversion. In the same manner, there is an inherent feeling that a nation is a noble and positive thing to be a part of, but it is not a positive thing to be a part of a sexual or racial group.

Grace Glueck: Yes, I think that's true, but one also has the feeling that women as a group don't really have a point of view. Blacks as a group really don't have a point of view. I've heard museum directors rationalize their decisions on these grounds. Isn't it demeaning psychologically to insist that they have a common point of view when you present them in a show?

Lois Jones Pierre-Noel: Much depends upon your jury and the problem is two-fold when it comes to women and black artists. In the past the trouble for blacks has been all white juries. Many of the black artists have been left out entirely for years. I have been painting for forty years and I am just now beginning to blossom. My last show at the Boston Museum of Fine Arts last April consisted of eighty-nine paintings. It was the first time that the Boston Museum had given the show to a black. And I happen to be a woman. And I just heard from someone, who's on the staff of the Boston Museum, that at a meeting of the trustees they said that my show was one of the best that they had had in many years. It was attended by thirty-three thousand people. But I can't tell you what I suffered and how hard it has been to get to this place when I'm about to retire from teaching at Howard University.

Perry Miller Adato: Recently I did a free program called Women's Film Festival on WNET 13, and Claudia Wilds, who made one of the most interesting feminist films called *Joyce at 34,* didn't want me to include this film in the program. Claudia, who is very close to the women's movement, said, "I don't feel that it should be part of the Women's Film Festival. I'll give permission, but why does it have to be shown only in this context?" The Women's Film Festival was very successful and now as a result of that there may be a National Women's Film Festival with thirteen programs if we can raise the money. Claudia wrote me a letter afterwards and told me that she had changed her mind; that the Women's Film Festival demonstrated that institutions which don't use women filmmakers could no longer say that they were not using them because there are none. The festival included at least sixty films of very high quality made by women and it got national attention.

Women artists, and I'm speaking specifically about women filmmakers because that's where my experience is, may have to accept the fact that if they want to get recognition they may have to be shown as part of women's film festivals. If these are successful, there won't be any need in the future for women's film festivals but this is a necessary first step and a very successful one too.

Lois Jones Pierre-Noel: How much of this is relevant to the black art movement? I like to participate in black art shows because I feel that it is necessary to establish our identity. But I hope this will not go on forever and that we will someday exhibit simply as artists.

Ann Snitau: I don't know if I agree. I certainly want to infiltrate the culture at large, but I also expect that that culture often responds to the political movement inherent in the infiltration. I do want to see myself as a woman artist and part of what I have to say has come from that identity. The idea of merging my identity with that of others simply does not satisfy me. I think of myself as a political writer.

Grace Glueck: Did you ever consider that you are a part and that your subject matter may in time become part of the larger male culture?

Ann Snitau: With basic changes in that culture!

Patricia Burnett: Can you give me some suggestions on how to put pressure on *The New York Times,* for instance, to cover women's shows? How can we influence glossy magazines to give us articles on women? How can we get critics to cover the shows that women are putting on?

Grace Glueck: My male colleagues reject the idea of going to a woman's show. "Oh god, a woman's show, I know just what it's going to be like." I've heard that plenty of times. If there were more women art reporters and critics on newspapers, more shows would be covered. That's what it amounts to. In all the areas where women operate there is a much greater sensitivity to a woman''s point of view. So the solution to get more viewers and to get more people to come to women's art shows is to get more women in those publications, and I mean women who are not ashamed to admit that they are women and that, yes, they do have a stake in the success of the movement generally. How you go about getting these institutions to hire women is something else again.

Betsy Damon: If women are involved in making imagery and reshaping our culture to a certain extent, then shows for women are absolutely necessary until people are taught to look at art in a different way. And I'm proud of those shows.

Clare Spark-Loeb: I would like to report just a little bit on the experience of women in Los Angeles where we are trying to build not only an interchange among women in the L.A. community but a national and international interchange within the feminist movement as well. We need more women writers from within the feminist movement. We cannot depend on people who have been conditioned by a different set of standards to write accurately about our work. We are trying to develop a constant interchange rather than competing for fame and status in the usual way in the art establishment. We are trying to work collaboratively and intel-

Apple Corps Drama Group, (Madison, Wis.); writers, directors and actresses who perform feminist works written by members of their own group.

lectually. And believe me, I do not underestimate the difficulty of overcoming our traditional needs for male approval. It is a great struggle to abstain from the avenues of validation by society but we are finding that the level of reward and approval that we get from each other and from women in Los Angeles is tremendous. I am proud to show with women, write with women, and I would just as soon devote the rest of my life to doing that. It's going to be a long struggle.

Athena Tacha Spear: There is nothing wrong, art historically speaking, with having women's shows rather than American artist's shows. The only difference is that women or blacks are a less cohesive group because they haven't had a chance to have a dialogue with each other. There has been a considerable number of black artist shows and women artist shows but they have all been token shows. Museums, once they've had one, wash their hands of it— they've fulfilled their duty. I think this effort should become institutionalized so that real consciousness can be created and a style can develop. I think it would be fruitful to develop a common approach that can then infiltrate the country.

Grace Glueck: In regards to the question of style, let me ask you a tough question. As a woman artist, how does your imagery differ from that of your male colleagues?

May Stevens: I can only say that what I am doing is very anti-establishment, very anti-authoritarian.

Linda Nochlin: Her imagery identifies the male phallus with the most brutal, insensitive political aspect of our society. It certainly is taken from a viewpoint that men would not take.

Grace Glueck: Do we feel that there really is a specific kind of women's art, a specific kind of women's imagery, that does try to come to terms with the male white world?

Audience Member: I am an actress and I think that the artist does not respond as a member of a group. I don't act in a feminist way, I act spontaneously. Perhaps it's politically important now to be concerned with these issues, but I question if we are going to be better artists because of it. I think art is a spontaneous thing that you work at to make it better.

May Stevens: I'm not sure that it's possible to respond or create art without consciousness of yourself as a woman. I think what actually happens is that you cut off some part of yourself because of an unawareness and this will show in your art.

Audience Member: Possibly, but you are not going to be a woman because you asked someone what a woman is. Maybe I'm limited right now, but from my objective response all I do is enact people. I see a person and I act her. I try to create her, I try to live her.

Grace Glueck: Maybe your field doesn't really offer the striking imagery that the visual arts have to offer.

Elizabeth Janeway: I would like to raise a question that has not come up at all and I raise it in total ignorance because this does not have to do with my field. We have not discussed at all the fact that a great deal of art is thought of by the individuals and by the museums who buy it, not as art but as an investment. And I would like to inquire what effect this has on the process of acquiring art for museums or individuals. I believe that such an emphasis expresses itself in a general evaluation of a painting as a painting.

Grace Glueck: That is a very good point because any art dealer will tell you a woman's art does not sell. I've heard that from Leo Castelli on down. Dealers are reluctant to take on women artists for that very reason and this has a great deal to do with museum shows because museums are tied in with dealers in the market place.

Big Daddy Paper Doll by May Stevens, acrylic, 1971. Lerner-Heller Gallery, New York.

Linda Nochlin: I would like to point out that men artists have never felt a reluctance to join together to make their position clear. There were Cubists. There were Neo-Impressionists. All the great movements that we think of are group names. While occasionally there was a woman among them, for the most part they were men artists who joined together not thinking to sacrifice their individuality but because they had some common aim. And I don't think that Monet or his peers were terribly worried about being thought of as Impressionists. They all kept exhibiting in those shows.

Grace Glueck: But they had a stylistic point of view.

Linda Nochlin: Yes, but they came together on that stylistic viewpoint as a rebellion against an established view. They interacted with each other. There was no impressionist style before a group of rebellious artists came together and little by little their style began to look alike. It was a very interesting phenomena.

It was not just an aesthetic issue with the Impressionists. When Monet went to the Louvre to paint and instead of painting a picture inside the Louvre, stood out on the balcony and painted contemporary Paris, he thumbed his nose at the old masters inside. He was making a gesture that was political as well as aesthetic. I don't think they are really separable.

A lot of these issues which are depicted as purely aesthetic, cozy, and apolitical in scholarly books are not really so apolitical or asocial. The aesthetic and the social are constantly interacting.

Valentina Litvinoff: What social needs can we fulfill in our communities as artists?

Elvie Moore: I tend to think that an individual is responsible to society. I think we have to remember that women also frequent the art museums, that part of our problem is that we ourselves are sexist. We have the constituency to pressure institutions to change. In order for the individual to have an expression there must be a power base. The institution will bend only with power.

May Stevens: I want to speak about this apparent conflict of the personal and political because I feel that I deal with it in my own work. I feel that both aspects are absolutely necessary for me, in an enriching and very fertilizing way. Good art can be made without that personal quality, but political input is not going to hurt it. □

VOLUNTEERING: IS IT WORTHWHILE?

Discussion Leader: Cynthia Pitts
Director, Training and Technical Assistance, Community Relations-Social Development Commission, Milwaukee, Wisconsin.

Cynthia Pitts: I would like to explain the contextual framework within which I operate—I see black people and in many cases women as victims in the society in which we live. I see the social order as needing to be changed and I see myself as a change agent. I see women as being involved in traditional institutions as well as in the development of alternative institutions. There are some women who feel that we need to be involved in developing institutions that speak to the needs of women or blacks, and there are other women who feel that we need to be where the power is now to bring about change. Perhaps we need to be in both places.

I define the volunteer as any unpaid person contributing human resources, money or technical resources to an endeavor—in this case, art. I see four roles for the volunteer: 1) The policy maker, an unpaid board member for example. 2) The technical support person, who contributes technical skills. 3) The artist who exhibits, displays or performs for no money. 4) The educator who provides the learning climate in which people can develop the skills to provide their own technical support system. The question of developing skills is essential when you are working in the development of alternative systems.

As we operationalize the rhetoric of a movement, whether it is the black movement or the women's movement or the welfare rights movement or whatever, we will find that the movement becomes less visible as it actually begins to deal with real forces. The volunteer has to deal with the climate in which he or she operates. If you are operating within a climate where the residents are denied resources and not involved in the decision-making for that community, your role is already cut out for you.

Volunteers can have power in three areas: 1) The allocation of resources such as time, money, exposure. Are these resources open or closed to women? 2) Decision-making. Are decisions imposed or are they self-determined? Do women participate in forming the decisions that are going to affect their lives? 3) Standard-setting. Who sets the norms? Who sets the standards by which exhibits are judged, for example? Who decides what roles actually exist for men and women—that's been set by somebody somewhere and those who are excluded from it or who the standards operate against certainly didn't set the standards.

Some woman may say, "I am the only woman on an all male jury and I operate on the basis of the given norm." In the black movement we call that assimilation. It means that the norms have already been set and we decide that we shall assimilate— that we shall adopt the norm, that we shall adopt the life style, that we shall adopt the values of the dominant culture. I think in the women's movement it means that we shall adopt the values and norms that have been set by men. The question becomes is there an experience that women share that is not a part of the masculine experience and I would say that possibly there is. So that experience should be a part, not the only part, but still a part of the norm-setting and standard-setting that exists.

Let's go to something concrete. Let's talk about volunteer participation on policy-making bodies.

Ann Day: Now I don't know if I'm on the track of what you're saying. Prior to this meeting I have never been involved in feminist situations of any kind. But I do serve as a volunteer on a policy-making board for the National Endowment for the Arts and I am the one woman on that board. This has just happened recently and it has been a very interesting situation because when I was first appointed to this board, I assumed that I was the token woman on that board; that they thought that they had better do something about women so they picked me and set me on the board. I got there to discover that in point of fact that was not the reason at all. They needed input from a civic and community oriented arts person rather than from a specific theatre type or a painter or whatever. I was being asked to act as precisely what I am, not as a woman, but as an individual who has had certain kinds of specific experience that they needed. Since I am a woman, I may put a female context onto some things, but that is basically not the role I see for myself on that board. Now, would a confirmed feminist feel that I should be working in a feminist way on that particular board?

Cynthia Pitts: I can't speak from the feminist framework but I can speak from my own movement's experience and from a question of power. The fact of only one woman on a board is in itself indicative of a problem. What I'm posing is that unless you in that volunteer role begin to examine the data that will show you how open or closed that board and its resources have been to women, then you run the risk of unconsciously participating in the oppression that is being brought against women.

Susan Certo: Are there decisions that you are making on that board that would in fact benefit women artists, women who are struggling artists in projects or as individuals that is not being done because there is no awareness of that struggle?

Ann Day: There's certainly no awareness of that struggle. Many applications come in to this board from women artists, men artists, arts groups. Women's arts organizations get exactly the same kind of handling as others. Now, it is true that if I were to see any inequity arise, I would naturally be inclined to speak for women as quickly as I could being the only one there, but the situation never arose.

Cynthia Pitts: There should be a body of information that actually gives boards such as the one you're on some insight into how the standards are benefiting or depriving women. How much of the organization's resources are actually going towards efforts for women? If the culture is establishing some myths as truths that affect the way women deal with themselves and with each other, then women's groups can speak to that. And if resources of your board are not being allocated in a way that allows for that kind of expression, women's groups should be providing you with the information instead of expecting you and other boards to have immaculate perception and know what the data is.

I brought up the role of the board member as a volunteer because those are the people who set the norms for how hired people are going to be treated, that is where salary scales and job classifications are determined. When we talk about salaries, hiring practices, banking policies, we're really talking about the resources that are available at an institutional level. One of the clear inequities visible to all of us is that many of those resources are closed to us as women and we're involved in the struggle to open those resources. It is often at the volunteer board level that decisions are made about the allocation of resources. In most movements the biggest struggle has been to get more resources. Without participation in the decision-making process, not only is the method paternalistic but the standards are defined for you. I would see us in a volunteer service role as being highly conscious not only of the percentage of women hired by the community or institution, but where the decisions are made and are women part of the decision-making process. And if you are there do you consciously see yourself as having to make those kinds of decisions because you are representing the ideas of the women's movement?

Conversations from Wingspread*

Dan Price (moderator): Ms. Freedman, do you feel that women have been taken advantage of as a result of the volunteer process which is helpful to so many museums and art institutes?

Doris Freedman: I think that the volunteer force of women has been invaluable to our institutions. Have they been taken advantage of? Maybe in today's world. I think we have to examine who is volunteering and why they are volunteering and what it is that they actually do. Private museums can't exist without their volunteer women. I think the entire role has been put down by those who don't really know the capabilities that volunteers bring to the particular service they render, especially in the field of fund-raising.

Dan Price: It has been suggested, as I am sure you are far more aware than I, that by volunteering women are forced into a mold, a feeling that their contribution is not worth money and consequently is not as worthy as a contribution made by men.

Doris Freedman: I feel personally that we just have to change that attitude.

Linda Nochlin: Why don't we just *change* and have men volunteers too? Why is it just women who are doing the volunteering?

Doris Freedman: I think it's obvious. The women who are doing the volunteering are primarily women who have leisure time, who are economically secure and want to do something which is a status-fulfilling job for them. So they do it. Some of the volunteers I know are worth their weight in gold. Yes, I think they should be paid after museums have reexamined the role that women play in such an institution.

May Natalie Tabak: I find volunteering, which seems very nice, demeaning to women. It's also a way of keeping women on the staff completely underpaid. It means

*This dialogue has been excerpted from a national radio program sponsored by The Johnson Foundation. The conversation included participants from the Conference on Women and the Arts.

Untitled by Susan Brenner (Olympia, Wash.), oil, 1970.

that they are doing for pleasure something you wouldn't allow done in any other field simply because it's socially rewarding. I don't like this kind of power.

Linda Nochlin: I'm just curious about why the pool of volunteers happens to be almost exclusively women. Why aren't a lot of those women professionals and their husbands the volunteers with the leisure time?

Doris Freedman: There are men who volunteer. I have a husband who spends three-fourths of his free time on our local school board. There are a lot of men who do this.

Linda Nochlin: But they are using their free time. The implication is that women of a certain class have nothing but free time whereas their husbands are engaged in important "professional" remunerative activity and that the pool of volunteers is exclusively women of a certain class who occupy themselves with this activity.

Doris Freedman: Are you saying that those women should go and seek jobs?

Linda Nochlin: No, I'm saying that society is organized in a very peculiar way and that it is women who turn out to be the volunteers and that it's men who have "real" jobs as opposed to volunteering. Because real jobs in our society are defined by the fact that they are paid.

Doris Freedman: The way in which that was said is a put-down. I think there are some enormously responsible positions held by women who are not paid for it by choice and who are really making an impact, especially in some of the civic organizations. I'm not saying it's right or wrong, and I agree with you that society has created this particular situation but I think we have to rethink with a little more dignity what that professional volunteer is all about.

May Natalie Tabak: To assign a professional volunteer dignity doesn't interest me as much as the professional job. If the job is an important job for which she is qualified and she doesn't need the money, then let her give the job to someone who *is* qualified and *does* need the money. Let her raise money to pay the qualified woman who needs it. You'd never dream of saying to a man, come work at a competent professional job and just contribute your time.

Doris Freedman: And what makes you think that people are saying this to women? These women are going ahead and giving of their time out of free, independent choice. I happen to use a lot of volunteers who I find invaluable. □

MEN AND WOMEN AS PARTNERS IN CHANGE

Discussion Leader: Allyn Roberts
Psychologist and author; head of Midwestern Psychological Services, Madison, Wisconsin.

Allyn Roberts: In order to understand the underlying basis of some of men's fear and emotional reaction to the women's movement, it is necessary to examine the problem in terms of its social and historical as well as its personal context—social and cultural because all men and women raised in Western society are at one time in their development brainwashed about what a man and a woman is. The other facet of the problem has its roots in the biologic, genetic and psychic being. I'm going to focus these remarks mostly on the latter.

I'd like to comment on some of the social and historical aspects as I see them. I see two major historical, psychological trends occurring since the time of the Industrial Revolution which are in part responsible for much of the human liberation movement of which women's liberation is one part. First, the revolution from reliance on external to internal authority; and second, a long cycle of historical process, which has only recently reached its apex, where the products and values of science have been gradually enthroned as the primary god before which human beings in this Western society have worshipped. There is evidence from many sources that Western humanity is becoming disillusioned with this god and is beginning to replace him with a value system which places more emphasis on relationship as opposed to faith for major satisfactions.

This country was established by people who were escaping the abuses of external authority and who felt that they were able to assume responsibility and authority for themselves. From the time of kings until now individuals everywhere have been saying to authorities and institutions, I want more self-determination. This is the meaning not only of the black movement but of the worldwide student uprising in almost all cultures in the past several decades. As the structures of authority and institutions are gradually yielding and being replaced with democratic values, those persons and groups which are losing power are upset. And, of course, the male sex is one of the groups that must yield power to women. Today men do not understand the necessity or the value to themselves in doing so. This is the major source of fear and conflict in their personal and professional relationships with women.

Thoughtful Westerners now realize that there is no utopia—we are now so mechanized and free from the old slaveries that we have undreamed of leisure at our disposal although we don't know what to do with it. We know that the solution for this alienation and disquietude lies in the direction of inner space, not outer space, and everywhere we see the new shoots sprouting

Sphere with Inner Form by Dame Barbara Hepworth. (Photo © by Dame Hepworth.)

forth. This conference, for example, the very sensitive and exploratory group movements, rap centers, meditation, even drugs, are part of the search away from the scientific and mechanical and external to the humanistic and relationship-oriented internal values. There is another name for this revolution. It is, I think, fair to call it the feminine revolution as well. And men are both perplexed and threatened by it.

What is the feminine revolution? It is essentially a turning of the tide toward a new direction of which you and I can already see the beginnings. Western culture since the time of the industrial-scientific revolution has been on a course which as a psychologist

Caracas by Nancy Grossman (New York).
Collection: Albert J. Petcavage.

I would term a masculine course. Periods of history and movements can be legitimately categorized psychologically as masculine or feminine. This masculine era, which is now at its apex turning point, is characterized by a mode of thinking which is primarily analytic, quantitative, specialized and outer-scene oriented. The feminine era into which we are entering would be characterized by a mode of thinking which incorporates elements of the above but which is basically more wholistically oriented, integrative, qualitative, inner-scene and relationship oriented. In the new era thought will come to be balanced by feeling—a true humanism.

Let's get more specific now. What are some of the main male fears in relation to working and living with women? One of these basic innate and perhaps even genetic fears is the fear of destruction. On the deepest psychological level the female principle is in the end the victor. Water eventually wears through rock, not the other way around. On some deep levels the masculine principle fears annihilation by the feminine principle. In the lower animal kingdom there are many examples of the female destroying the male, never the other way around.

Another fear which I think we men universally experience at some time in our lives is the fear of our own male inadequacy. The male principle, while it appears on the surface to strut and show its muscle and display its certainty and strength, often on deeper analysis is found to have feet of clay. No weakness or inadequacy can be tolerated so when weakness is recognized we may become ruthless in attempting to suppress it or we go to elaborate measures to hide it even from ourselves. And one of our seeming weaknesses is that we need women. Woman has learned that she is a danger to man because of the weakness he finds in himself when he is with her. He comes to her at his peril for she can soften him. I think we men are ashamed of that unless we are very secure.

We judge ourselves by our productivity and our achievement. To achieve and to gain recognition for our achievement becomes terribly important to us because we are not capable of the very highest form of creation —to create another human being. We often guard the gates to our own achievement and we become quite worried when she whom we know to be capable of that highest achievement enters into that which we feel to be our domain. Again unless we are quite secure, we may suddenly try to strike her out or relegate her to a position of containment and safety. We have devised some very subtle ways to put her down.

We thought for many ages that woman's sole function was to give sustenance and love. We have different standards for interpreting non-agreement if it comes from women than if it comes from our male colleagues. We often interpret disagreement from a woman to mean lack of love and we may panic about that. Women are partly responsible for this because they have so often played the game of agreement even when they didn't believe it in order to give man what he wants.

Men are afraid of the irrational and the contradictory. We have absolutely got to make sense of everything, whereas women seem to be more comfortable in the realm of the contradictory—more comfortable on that knife edge of paradox. We men badly need to learn this secret because a world without tolerance of the irrational is, I think, a sterile and dangerous world.

We feel uncomfortable and inferior to you in the realm of relationships. To some extent psychologically the present increasing concern with human behavior and with relationships between people is usually a more feminine concern and is one more indication of society's present gender. An important part of relationships in which men are frequently awkward concerns giving and yielding. Men must learn some things which women presently know much better, how to live for others, how to subordinate achievement and progress to deeper human goals. Men must learn one of the very things which so many women today appear to be in conflict about.

We are afraid of feeling and emotion. Men are taught to give heed to their heads, not to their hearts. As a result, men often do not know what they feel which sometimes surprises women. In work situations, for example, dealing with a woman often means facing feelings and we don't want to do that. So we feel threatened by women and

vice versa. When this threat remains unstated and unresolved, it translates into a tremendous waste of human energy and potential.

How can we resolve this problem? With solutions that are part of the greater social solution: women in organized fashion pushing for equal rights, conferences such as this one to help focus and define problems, more situations for genuine dialogue between the sexes. Men want that although they are also very much afraid of it. Why haven't women taken more initiative in creating and organizing more informal situations where dialogue can take place, both in their jobs and in their other roles? This

M. L. Sweeney by Nancy Grossman.
Collection: Mrs. Gates Lloyd.

initiative has got to come from women but the social attack is, of course, only a partial solution. Just as the solution to the problem of war is not in wearing buttons and carrying placards, but rather in learning to face and then eradicate the violence in our individual lives. The solution for men and women is to resolve that aspect of the conflict in themselves.

It's within ourselves that we can be doing something about every moment. When this change transpires, when we come to terms with the person within us, only then can we become whole and fully creative persons. An idea we seem to be discovering here is that people in the arts, male or female, are closer to androgyny. They seem closer to a wholeness than is true in some other areas. It seems that creativity comes from a unified whole mind.

It's time to open up the discussion. What do you think?

Linda Heddle: Recently at another kind of meeting a woman psychologist gave the advice that women should refuse to do all the emotional work for men any more. This would force men to see the emotional situation and recognize what emotions are in practice.

Kay Clarenbach: This strikes me as punitive. I can think of ways of teaching other than to withhold my own humanity by not responding in ways that come naturally to me. I have seen parents who are as non-sexist as anybody of our generation can be and they have taught both their male and female offspring to feel, face, and express emotions. So I think that it's not an impossible kind of task.

Linda Heddle: I did not mean that women should stop interacting with men or that they should withhold a giving of themselves, but that they should react from their own position rather than from that of the man.

Allyn Roberts: I think you have to make a judgment about whether the other person is hearing. If he's able on some level to begin to hear you, then it can be a very constructive thing to withhold but if the threat level is too much I feel that it would not only shut the person off but defeat your broader goal of teaching the person something.

Ann Snitau: You want unity very much. I also hope that we can all achieve it by understanding. But unity comes at the end of a very long period of time when in fact one is not unified. Objective conditions like money and power and time and childbirth obstruct unity. I have been the token woman in an English department and there were times when unity would have been a bit of a lie. Sometimes we were all very friendly, but the fact of the matter was that the power was unequal and the feeling of freedom was unequal and the number was unequal. In this kind of situation, you can't for a minute believe that if women just understood what is within themselves the problem would be solved. Men should perhaps accept a phase of disunity where a woman would say, "No, I cannot accommodate you, I cannot make you comfortable in this situation any more." It needn't be punitive but it can be an expression of self, an expression of the reality of the present level. Then, through struggle we can get some kind of unity at a later stage. Negative emotion should be valued too. I'm afraid of negative emotions as much as anyone, and yet I learned from the women's movement that I was going to have to find out about them in order to become myself and to have honest relationships with men.

Allyn Roberts: And it must be terribly important for many women to be able to express that negative emotion—it can be a self-enhancing experience.

Kay Clarenbach: Expressing a negative emotion is not withholding an emotional response.

Ann Snitau: I feel if I express a negative emotion then men will have to change. Men and women have to be enemies at some stage to discover that very hard to understand fact that negative feelings can be very creative, they can be a stage of learning for us.

Valentina Litvinoff: To say that our enemy is man is not only self-defeating, it is not true. All of the men I know are victims of exactly the same set of circumstances that has made us feel victimized and unfulfilled. The only difference is that it's more pronounced with us and the conditions which made us the victims also use the male as an instrument to keep us down. This is a complex situation but if we understand it we begin to realize that the enemy is not man any more than woman is the enemy to man. Something else is the enemy and we've got to find out what it is so we can both join hands in the struggle to make ourselves better human beings.

Allyn Roberts: Yes, it isn't two separate problems: it's one problem but it shows itself in different faces. To clarify, I was attempting to say that men are not comfortable with their dependence on anything, but women generally are more comfortable with dependence than men are.

Kay Clarenbach: A lot fewer women are comfortable with dependence than used to be.

Ludmilla Bollow: I've had a great difficulty in writing men's characters; I find it very hard to even define a man's character. I do think that women are much more open in their feelings. It's easier to write from a woman's viewpoint than to define a man because men are elusive about their inner thoughts.

Allyn Roberts: Can you look at the man within you to get some clues?

Ludmilla Bollow: Well, I've come to that but I've had a very difficult time doing it. As a writer you have to understand men or you cannot write about life.

Edward Kamarck: Allyn, to what degree are fears that men have regarding their relationships with women conditioned by the sexist roles in which society shapes itself? I think this is really the crucial question. I don't think the fears are inherent. I think they are the result of conditioning and that both men and women are victimized by sexist roles; both similarly face problems of breaking through the molds of enforced barbarisms, the violence, the violated sensibilities which come from these sexist roles. We do not live in a human society. We live in a society which does do violence to our

Diary of a Mad Housewife, directed by Eleanor Perry (New York).

sensibilities and which shapes us in unfortunate ways and makes for unfortunate patterns of conduct and expectations.

Allyn Roberts: My own response is that the social factors are overwhelmingly more important here but I'm not willing to disregard that there may be some effect of a quarter of a billion years of men functioning primarily as the hunter and women functioning primarily as a nest-builder and what this has done to the evolutionary, genetic process. We shouldn't out of our emotional feelings cut off our minds to this possibility.

Ann Snitau: If I were your patient and I had to deal on any level, even a subliminal level, with the idea that for eons I had been the nest builder and you had been the hunter, it would be extremely confusing to me. It would be a disintegrating, negative influence in my life, no matter how sympathetic you might be to my struggles. It's a dangerous over-simplified view. We have more anthropological models to work with than that.

Allyn Roberts: I'm hearing a fair amount of anger towards a point of view which is not really my point of view. I'm stating a point of view that I think is prevalent among a large segment of men. I can understand your anger because you cope with this attitude every day.

Barry Schwartz: I think what we are talking about is deprograming. I think deprograming can occur, but you cannot do it alone. You need help because you need feedback. I am not the best judge of my impact. If a person is not a male chauvinist, he will make the commitment to incorporate feedback. I insist on relationship. I want relationship more than anything else.

Barbara Coffman: But it's breaking the barrier to get to that.

Harriet FeBland: Isn't what is really necessary is more education? After all, here we are at a conference of women with a few males. It is a very important beginning but it's only a beginning. What we are really talking about is re-educating society, not only men but women. How shall women now act, how shall men react? With my own two sons I see a difference now. It's great to watch them react to their girlfriends and see how they're interpreting the girls' reactions to themselves. They are far more feminist in their thinking than perhaps my husband. Somewhere along the line my sons were educated properly. It's great to have the education happen at this very high level. But educating society is much more than formal education. When we talk about all of society—all males and females—then we've got to get more people involved in this education. We have to involve the writers of books, the writers of newspapers and magazines, all the arts.

Allyn Roberts: What are some of the most effective deconditioning approaches?

Kay Clarenbach: I think one is to reward and approve non-pig behavior in men. A lot of us have an angry tendency just to label the chauvinist statement or gesture or action when we see it and rightfully so, but I think at the same time we should encourage non-chauvinist behavior and say this is my idea of a real man, not someone who can drop a bomb or kick a football.

Mary Michie: To point out to men who among them is liberated.

Valentina Litvinoff: Men will benefit by women's liberation. Someone pointed out that they are the losers, that it's a form of competition, but this isn't so at all, is it? It is a two-way thing. A segment of the population cannot be subjected and deprived by another segment without having the instruments of the deprivation lose a great deal of their humanity. I think those fears which you described would vanish much faster if men could see that women's liberation creates a kind of woman who would be more loving and a better companion for him and that his own humanity would blossom as a result.

Elvie Moore: This may happen depending on the woman; it may not happen depending on the woman. The woman may present a very viable economic threat. When we're talking about social change, we're talking about a whole multi-faceted problem that women's liberation is going to present in society. When you're moving towards a more humanistic society, you're going to be changing institutions so fast that you do not even know that you are changing them and you are bound to come into great conflicts with males. They have a reason to be threatened because their economic base and how they have related to that economic base is going to be threatened. I would like to know if we feel we can really deal with the kind of impact that we as women can generate in society. Can we deal with the changes that men may have to go through, that we may have to go through? Can we deal with money? What does it mean when you are a successful professional artist making $25,000 and your husband is making $10,000 a year when the society is gauged on the image of economics? How are you going to deal with that in a family scene? How is your husband going to deal with it, is he going to stay home and cook and clean? The roles within the situation are going to be coming into juxtaposition. Are you going to have to say I'm going to be an artist and I'm going to be single? There are so many questions that we have to deal with when we're talking about being a woman professional, a woman artist. Any man would be threatened. I feel threatened by just having to confront what the future may offer.

Allyn Roberts: What's your anwer to it?

Elvie Moore: I have no answer.

Valentina Litvinoff: Some of the changes you mentioned will probably have to come through modifications and changes in the economy so that men and women aren't pitted against each other as they are now.

Doris Freedman: On the basis of economics, what is to assure that the positive elements that you talk about in the feminine principle will be maintained once women do attain more powerful, more influential positions? Will they not perhaps adopt those so-called male principles?

Allyn Roberts: It would seem if you look at what is happening in society that the extremes are becoming less, are they not? We see more and more men becoming comfortable with things that were viewed even a generation ago as female characteristics. How can we hasten this process even more?

Ann Snitau: Yes, I see a change. The younger student men seem to be much more open to these notions and there is cultural movement, but I think we have to deal with the hard part—with the economic threat and the question of how men can be convinced to give up power. How can androgyny take place if we don't accept the idea of political struggle?

Bonnie Cashin: All we talk about is power. Power is within yourself. It's educating yourself and opening up your own mind so you are a more creative person. I really get impatient with women who spend all their time talking and no time developing. You have x amount of time and x amount of energy in your life and if you spend all that energy talking about how you're put down, you have no time to use that energy for anything constructive. I mean you've got to rise above it, you've got to rise and see things in a comprehensive way. You all sound as though you've had horrible experiences. I really don't see it as horrible experiences.

Kay Clarenbach: You don't see a dehumanized world that needs a lot of change?

Bonnie Cashin: I don't. I'm a successful business woman. I've worked since I was sixteen years old. I came from a poor but intellectual family.

Kay Clarenbach: And it doesn't distress you to see Watergate?

Bonnie Cashin: Of course it does, but that doesn't have anything to do with my creativity. That's another facet of life. It has nothing to do with what I produce. I feel if I fulfill myself and use every vestige of creativity within me and view all of the problems in a creative way, then I've done pretty well.

Kay Clarenbach: Yes, but this session is dealing with social change and how men and women can be partners in social change.

Bonnie Cashin: It's dealing with social change and my work is in social change— it's freeing woman in a certain area of life so she can get on with the marvelous business of living. I can't take it all on so I do my own little tiny part.

Roberta Meyer: You use this word creativity and you say that we should use our creative energies to find out in what direction we should be moving in. Do you realize that the nature of creativity is moving from the known to the unknown? We can only deal with what we do know. And we are doing a creative thing in trying to find out what is in the future for us. That's right in the heart of the creative process. We cannot formulate that. □

CHANGING THE VALUES AND PRACTICES OF CULTURAL INSTITUTIONS

Discussion Leader: Lois Jones Pierre-Noel
Artist and Professor, Department of Art, Howard University.

Lois Jones Pierre-Noel: As a black woman I am naturally interested in equality of opportunity. I would say that one-half of all contemporary work shown should be by women and one-half of single artist shows should be by women. Boards of trustees, educational programs and so forth should equitably represent the races and sexes. And one of the best strategies for bringing about change is to establish lines of communication between Black, White, Puerto Rican, Native American, Chicano, Oriental artists and women artists. What procedures have worked for Blacks, for example, and can similar ones work for women?

Vivienne Anderson: What are the strategies whereby you translate what you want to get into the life blood of these institutions which are for the most part very rigid, sometimes decadent, and where the power base is strong and the leadership resistant to change? As long as the policies remain polarized, the policy makers remain polarized from those who want change. I believe that the polarization has to be broken and the forces have to begin to think together and to change together.

Betsy Damon: Unfortunately an institution can easily exhaust any number of individuals who might have the energy to attack it.

Vivienne Anderson: I don't think that individuals can necessarily attack the institution.

Ruth Milofsky: Institutions regularly outweigh the disturbers. They make some minor concession, they wait for the people to forget about it or to graduate or go away and then they maintain the status quo. There has to be some very serious continuing effort.

Kay Johnson: The working classes faced this long ago and their answer was to be unionized.

May Stevens: For women? If it's a faculty union, for example, the women will be more than outnumbered by the men.

Kay Johnson: Well, you may decide, as a relevant part of your contract, making the executive body half women—you negotiate from this premise.

Perry Miller Adato: I think this is an important point. If you formed a union of faculty members or, in my experience, an association of the producers, the male producers will outnumber the female producers by eight or nine to one. How are you going to get those men to fight for fifty percent of jobs to be given to women when it's against their own interest?

Kay Johnson: Faculties face these problems already and liberal as men on faculties like to say they are, they are not when it comes to this question.

70

The Money Eaters by Miriam Beerman (New York), oil, 1970.

Lorraine Gross: But some of these problems have been solved. The laws now state that you *must* have greater proportions of women on your faculty than previously, so this year they are seeking women.

Pat Clark: They have affirmative action programs at the universities now that are supposed to be doing great things but they simply protect the institution. The affirmative action person is usually set up as the buffer between the women and the university to protect the university laws. Really, it's a very tenuous position and we must admit that we are "tokens." In order to really become active we have to become *politically* active.

Betsy Damon: I think we're in a period of "deep tokenism." Every woman in this room would be deluding herself if she thought that real progress has been made. We are in a crisis moment because there are so many women now receiving opportunities for themselves and having their consciousnesses raised, but the concessions won are tokens. Every institution has a one-woman show. Vassar has one, the cultural center has one, and there were only two more women represented in the Whitney annual in spite of the enormous protest that went on a year before.

Cornell has no more women tenured faculty than it had fifteen years ago but it has affirmative action. It hired a black woman to solve two problems and that poor woman is in such a terrible position that she will leave. She shouldn't stay. It's a burden to her. We really have to conceive of ourselves as a political body and as a grassroots movement using everything from law to an aggressive movement. But we have to remember that the law will only work with aggressive movement.

Margaret Mahoney: We should think about strategy in the true sense of the word, about what we want and how we are going to get it. The basic issue in change is to know where the power lies. We have to inform ourselves about where decisions are made—within single institutions, within the overlapping institutions, the federal sector or the state sector. I would tell you as a devil's advocate that it is a waste of time to say that you do not want to associate with women's groups or be in a woman's show or that you do. The issue is, if you want to get from A to B, you're going to have to decide how to do that. As women one of our strategies should be precisely to have shows on women and on black women because that's the way to get things started, names into papers, names advanced. One of the problems that university people tell me all the time in every field is that we can't find women. Well, in one way, it's true. It's extremely difficult to find a talent. It's exciting for me to come here and see so much talent—it usually is not collected.

Perry Miller Adato: We have to recognize that what we are talking about is power and influence. Women are afraid of the word "power." Changing things means having influence. In four years there has been an enormous change in the visibility and the characterization and the image of the black on television and film. There were certain things the blacks did. First of all, they raised the consciousness of black people. When we first heard "Black Power," all of us, including myself, were very frightened. What were they going to do? And then we began to realize that they weren't talking about taking over the power. They were talking about *sharing* the power.

It was easier with blacks because blacks knew they were being discriminated against. It's harder with women because a lot of women who are not in this room do not know that they are discriminated against, do not realize that they have a subordinate position.

Lois Jones Pierre-Noel: Really, one of the most important tools for change is harassment. I mean you really can be effective. You must unify. That's what we did as blacks. We have the National Conference of Artists and we *unify* and then demand, and harass, and embarrass.

Ruth Milofsky: I have the impression that all institutions are very sensitive to bad publicity.

Margaret Mahoney: But it depends upon what role you play and where the visibility is. Wouldn't it be best for us to try to generate specific ideas and then go back and see what we can do? I think that litigation, for example, is extremely important. It's only one point but it ought to happen all the time. Every time you have a case it ought to be brought into a litigation system. There are about twenty, thirty, or fifty mechanisms and you've got to get them out on the floor so that we can understand what they are.

Vivienne Anderson: We may get a series of little victories which are very crucially important but until we actually crash the policy-making level we don't get anywhere. I have observed that there are people in top policy-making positions who have a very sincere commitment to equality for women, a very sincere conviction that that commitment is real. They really believe it, but there is a big difference between this conviction and their own personal sincerity and what actually happens within that institution. We have to become a part of the top echelon policy-making instrument.

Those forces that you are talking about garnering have to address themselves to the highest level. We have in New York today in our own department—the education department—a task force working on this problem. When we started out we were all a part of an amorphous bureaucracy and we started out with a very philosophical stance. Not one of us thought that we ought to ask the Commissioner of Education to let us sit as a watch-dog committee on the appointments that are made in the policy-making echelon. After a while though we finally did ask for statistics. The position paper which was issued by the state board of regents and the Commissioner espoused a very sincere theory of equality for women in curriculum and employment, etc., but when we asked our personnel division to give us statistics on the appointments that had been made from the issuance of the paper (which was one year ago) up to the present date, we found that at the bureau chief level and above we had thirty-three appointments in that period of time, three of which were women. One of those was a lateral transfer, technically a new appointment but we didn't consider it so. At that point we changed our entire stance. We submitted a specific policy recommendation which was that the appointments made in the G-27 and above jobs (bureau chief and above) must be fifty percent women. It came back to us again and we modified it to thirty percent with a repertoire system that has to be scrutinized by the task force at given periods of time. That has been accepted.

Die by Faith Ringgold (New York), oil, 1967.

Recently we had an open-door session in the department. We asked people to come in and talk about this problem. Not one man came, but fifty women came. It was a very interesting, very informal discussion. At the beginning of the session three women from the governor's staff joined us. In talking with them after the meeting they told me that they had pointed out to the governor that the situation in the departments of state was unconscionable and they had actually persuaded him to be receptive to this problem. They said that within one year they are going to visit every department of state and hold open hearings in every department. At the same time they are building a "talent pool," they are getting résumés, because as was pointed out before the first thing that is always said is: "Oh sure, we can appoint women to top jobs but we can't get any qualified women." Well, they are going to have a "bank" available and, she said, "By the end of this year the departments of state will be screaming for women because they will be *pushed* into a position where they have to."

Perry Miller Adato: That is just exactly the point. I think the key operative phrase is "pushed into a position where they have to."

Margaret Mahoney: I'd put first on the list of priorities information gathering. Without the data there will be no platform with which to begin.

Betsy Damon: The evaluation of the artist's work is subjective however. And all the pressure in the world and all of the objective evaluation won't insure that museums will include certain types of art work. The very exclusion of certain kinds of art work is debilitating to us. It's debilitating to the artist.

Barbara Manger: Are these institutions worth fighting to get into or can some of our energy be directed toward forming alternative institutions? In many cases that is a much more profitable use of energy, time, and effort than batting our heads against the wall.

Margaret Mahoney: You really haven't changed the system then.

Perry Miller Adato: I don't believe the answer in media, for example, is for women to make their own films and make their own tapes although I suggested that as one of the things that should be done. I don't think that we can just give up the other ninety-five percent of the film and television world which affects our children. We really have to make our own personal choice. Do I want to start an alternative small outlet or do I want to get into an established structure? We have to do both and we have enough women to do both if we raise their consciousness.

May Stevens: What is needed is a national, powerful Women in the Arts Committee. In the peace movement there never was just one organization but all worked together on specific strategies. I think people who have been to Washington know that they will never forget that experience.

Fannie Hicklin: I have been interested in a number of comparisons which you have made with the black movement and it is a little upsetting to see that after you have spent only three years in the movement, some of you are despairing. We spent a hundred years and we did not despair. There was no one organization—we had Urban League, NAACP, SLAVE, CORE. You have had things rather comfortable, most of you, and your consciousness has suddenly been aroused. Our consciousness went on over a long period of time. And it was a matter of knowing that one plugged away wherever one could. And that meant as an individual or as a member of a group or whatever. What's three years in terms of one's individual life or in terms of a raise or in terms of a group? And so now that you have had your consciousness suddenly aroused, you have become irritated and you expect an immediate terminal. How long has it taken some of you to accept blacks? You may not yet really accept them but you suddenly want to be accepted as women. I want to be and I recognize the legitimacy of all that you have said but I think that you are not being totally realistic and practical because you don't get people to change immediately.

Betsy Damon: The women's movement has been around for a hundred years too. □

Wind Intervals by Phyllis Mark (New York), kinetic sculpture turned by wind, presently located at Carl Shurz Park, 86th Street and East End Avenue in New York City.

THE ETHICS OF POWER

Discussion Leader:
Sister Mary Austin Doherty
*Professor of Psychology, Alverno College,
Milwaukee.*

Sister Mary Austin Doherty: Most of us women have a very difficult time dealing with the question of power. The ethics and the use of power cause some very serious guilt feelings. The reasons for that seem to be that in our society there are different definitions of power attributed to the two sexes. The power attributed to men is direct, physical, effective. The power that is usually attributed to women is an indirect kind of power which supposedly manifests itself in manipulative or exploitative rather than beneficial ways. This is just a paradigm of what happens with other concepts in our society—we divide them in order to attribute one aspect of it to men and one aspect of it to women. Those of us who are artists and who are interested in women as artists and their contributions must learn to define power out of our own lived experience as women, rather than accepting this attribution of power as it is often laid upon us. What does it mean for a woman to exercise power as an individual, as a member of a group, or within the group itself?

Ilona Kombrink: In my profession as a performer it's very difficult to say how power is given because in music you have delegated positions of power. A first singer in an opera house has a certain unquestioned position of power as an individual. It's different when you sing in a chamber group, however. I find that power does begin with oneself.

Nancy Knaak: Several years ago one of the administrators on our campus said rather angrily, "Power is worthless unless it's

Marian Anderson. Courtesy: Metropolitan Opera.

used," which is an idea I haven't really made up my mind about yet but it seems to me that power might be available to draw on without necessarily always being used. Another male colleague once suggested that in my own appearances before the university administrative council in discussions on affirmative action I should never go in without telling my friends on the committee ahead of time what I would say to make sure that they would not attack me. And my argument was, "I've known these people for twenty years; and if I can't talk to them about an idea without getting all tied up in knots, nothing will be accomplished." And I'm not going to play the game in the old manipulative way. Naturally, I think my approach is the ethical one.

Vera Mowry Roberts: I have always felt that power corrupts and absolute power corrupts absolutely. This can be historically demonstrated over and over again. I'm a theater historian by scholarly persuasion and so I'm always taking a historical viewpoint. One of the difficulties in the status of women historically has been that they have had so little direct power. I think it's a concept that we even have some difficulty in dealing with. Does power mean being able to tell other people what to do and see that it gets done? Does it mean the plotting of solutions to problems and having the plan that everybody adopts?

In my own experience, in the positions of authority and responsibility that I have held, I have found that I was indeed able to move groups. And I have come to believe that the art of persuasion is the greatest power an individual can possess because it takes into account the fundamental worth and dignity of the other persons with whom you are dealing. I think that as women move more rapidly and in greater numbers into positions of power we are faced with the question: Are we afraid of power? If we are in the decision-making seats, we must take the responsibility for those decisions. That's pretty scary.

Patricia Kerr Ross: My responsibility is to conduct a university-wide arts program and my work puts me in a very unique position. Since I'm part of the central administration, one of very few women in a very large organization, I think I have an advantage

because amidst difficult, almost unsolvable problems, I represent the arts. And the arts have a wholesome power, a positive image. Somehow the area that I represent is not a terribly difficult problem area to the administrators I deal with. I think I have power because of the fact that they're disarmed by the arts; because the artist is seen as a very positive force in the State University of New York. I don't want to use that power accidentally. I don't want to make the mistake of not being absolutely aware of what I'm doing so that I lose the advantage in my own situation.

Athena Tacha Spear: Personally, I am not worried about power. I have had it whenever I wanted it and I am not afraid of taking the responsibility for it. I am most interested in the aspect of women as a group acquiring more power, but without imitating the power structure of men and without becoming a part of the same corrupt system.

Elizabeth Janeway: If we just say power corrupts, we might as well say that because fire burns, we won't use fire.

Clare Spark-Loeb: George Bernard Shaw said that it is fools who corrupt power and I'm with him. I want all the power I can get so that I can go to the beach with a clear conscience.

May Natalie Tabak: I can reject power or accept it as a private citizen but my relations to power as a novelist are completely different. I have no ethic to express as a novelist because I cannot let an ethic come between me and my character's action. I want to know about power for my character so that I can free the part of myself that is very rigid, very ethical, and a terrible bore. As a novelist I'm interested in the power that women have as social creatures at a dinner party or a tea party or their status in the community. I'm interested in the power of gossip. Several of you mentioned the power of persuasion which is also the power of seduction—it's a subtle difference. Seduction is merely a corrupt form of persuasion.

I have one more point. Why do we sound so pathetic when we talk of a woman having only indirect power; we are full of admiration for the prime minister who's manipulating the whole country and the king and the queen by indirect power. We feel there's nothing pathetic about his role.

Faith Ringgold: I'd like to know quite a few things about power. I'm not afraid of it; I like it, but I don't have any. What I do have is the power that I have over myself. I associate power with freedom and I feel freedom within myself. I live in a hostile world and I feel powerless in relating to other people and to the world, but inside myself I feel free and powerful.

May Stevens: I'm an artist and I'm very aware of what I don't like in the structures which exist into which I would have to move in order to succeed professionally on the level that I would desire.

Rose Slivka: I never knew I had power until they, the people on the outside, told me that I had power. I guess I was not conscious of it because I assumed that the opposite of power is helplessness and that I think is corrupting. And so I realize that I have got

to face the power needs, that is, the freedom to do what I want to do with my ideas and, to me, that is power.

Linda Nochlin: I'm interested in three aspects of power. First of all, I think it's not power that corrupts but weakness that corrupts. The second thing is the notion of justice in relation to power. I don't think that women should have any obligation to be better than a man. I feel it is being the good girl scout to feel that women must have moral superiority. When you're weak you can feel morally superior because you don't have to feel responsible. I hope that we can change the power structure, but I don't think that it's women's obligation. I think women should have power in the interest of justice. The more groups that have access to power, the more we have a just society. It might be a very wicked society, but at least more of us will be responsible for it, good or bad. And third: I'm interested in the relational aspects of power—power as a kind of dynamic relation. It's not some hard and fast lump that you

Untitled sculpture by Linda Howard (New York).

can clutch to yourself; it's how you relate to the world.

Sister Mary Austin Doherty: How can women be powerful considering these notions about the kinds of power we already have and the hazards built into the way it is currently exercised? How can we build into our concern the responsibility inherent in power and remain true to ourselves as women?

Linda Heddle: When individual women get in positions of power, administrative positions, directorships on boards, they have power. How do they exercise that power? When women get in these positions they are often accused of becoming just like men.

Athena Tacha Spear: Women don't have to prove that they're better than men but why not learn from their mistakes. I'm very bothered by the fact that many individual women and groups of women who acquire power within the movement seem to turn it against others. I think that's imitating the examples of how power has been used so far within male-dominated societies and I would like to see alternatives to that.

Faith Ringgold: Until the women's movement becomes a movement that crosses class lines, it's no different than any other movement with a narrow focus. Actually, there is no amount of conversation or instruction or workshops that is going to stop powerful women from doing powerful negative things if they get a chance, and they will get a chance if the mass of women are not exercising their own individual powers to keep themselves free and to keep people from controlling them. The society itself has to prevent powerful people from controlling it. If more people wanted to change things and more people got involved, there would be no room for the all-powerful single individuals.

Clare Spark-Loeb: I think we need to deal with the specific instance of who's using power for what ends in what context. If we organized our educational systems from early childhood toward collective ends, toward changing society, toward responding to all kinds of human needs instead of perpetuating the power structure which exists, all of our institutions of education would be totally different. Our relationship to thought and action would be different.

At what point in child rearing does the idea of thought and action become separated? Don't we, after we get certain kinds of knowledge, diminish our humanity if we don't act on that knowledge? Don't we have to turn off vital parts of our being by not acting? So many of us have so much invested in our lives that it's truly going to be a struggle to change. I'm terribly concerned with changing elementary schools, nursery school education, child-bearing practices, getting control of mass media so that people who don't have access to these advanced institutions can benefit from them. But we have to also not be afraid of the radical implications that this will mean. It's not a joke and it's a lifelong commitment; and we're very likely to be knocked off. I'm not so sure that all of this talking should be going on in public frankly. I find it bizarre that women should be talking about tactics on television shows. I'm sorry when women accede to formats not of their own choosing and are used in a way which makes spectacles of them. In talking about power, we should always be very specific and always evaluate each situation in terms of politics. Are we sharing power or are we grabbing power? Are we giving to the art system or are we using our power to help others get power faster themselves? We have to accept the fact that we will never devise a social system where every person gets his or her way.

Linda Nochlin: We neglected one aspect of power—that it is often very boring, annoying and burdensome. This often causes conflict in the best sort of people because they simply don't want to waste their time with it even though they know they might do something awfully good through it.

Athena Tacha Spear: When you have power, you have all the chores that go along with it. But, by distributing power, you can avoid this.

Linda Nochlin: Once people have a good taste of the burdensome aspects, they bcome much happier to share power and that does not mean delegating it. In actuality power is not its own reward except for certain, very specific types of people. Often it's simply the goal in view that makes certain people want power at all. It's not an abstract thing, it's related to the goal and related to other people. □

HOW FEMINISM IN THE ARTS
CAN IMPLEMENT CULTURAL CHANGE

Anomie by Joyce Treiman (Pacific Palisades, Cal.), oil, 1971-72.

by Linda Nochlin
Professor of Art History, Vassar College.

The question I shall deal with is: "How can feminism in the arts implement cultural change: defining aims and developing a philosophy to deal with the outer and the inner realities of women. The goal is to resolve a conflict between ingrained attitudes and new possibilities and develop a plan for translating philosophy and aims into practical reality in cultural institutions." This is a rather large order. The best way of approaching it is a way that I've learned from the woman's movement—that is, in terms of my own personal experience.

Since I am an art historian and since art history, and art, are cultural institutions, I should like to tell you something about the way feminism has led me to question and reformulate my own position in relation to the arts and to history itself. Feminism has been an enormous intellectual, spiritual, and practical breakthrough in my life as a human being and as a scholar. Since, however, I don't distinguish between the self and society and don't see them as opposites— I see them, rather, as totally interconnected —in talking about myself, I'm talking about a social issue. Unlike many of the other people here, I don't see a basic conflict between the individual and the social group. The self seems to me a piece of the social group that happens to be enclosed in a certain boundary of skin and bone and has incorporated a great many values and ideals of the larger society. Even the feelings that one thinks of as being most personal are ultimately gotten from somewhere. And what is that somewhere? I don't think it's nature in the raw. It's the particular historical, social and cultural situations that one is born into. And in turn, the individual or the self is constantly acting upon and modifying and changing the social group so that self and society or individual and institution are not hard and fast opposing entities but really a kind of process in a constant state of mediation and transaction. Therefore when I talk of my personal experience, I'm not opposing it to the nature of history, to the nature of an intellectual discipline. I see them as part of the same sort of structure and, therefore, I think any one individual's life and experience can be a paradigm for the whole, can stand as an example of the whole. It's not my little personal life as opposed to every one out there or even to this country or to this historical moment that I'm really talking about.

How in effect does feminism have an influence on the way I look at art history? Or, to make the issue even stronger, how does the notion of feminism transform for me the institution of art, the nature of art, and the whole way I look at history? I'll give you some examples because I think they are useful.

One of the primary notions that we have about art is the notion of genius. Art, great art, is created by great geniuses. And these geniuses are in some way mythical beings—different from you and me, more valuable than you and me—whose products are in some way inestimably richer and more important than anything that you or I could produce. And the genius who is looked up to by our society as the very apex of human achievement is seen, *par excellence,* as the individual, the one who is set apart from or rebels or is in some way elevated above the mass of ordinary human beings.

When I began to be interested in feminism and when I started looking into the actual, concrete historical situations in which art was created or could be created, I found some very interesting things. Far from being totally unpredictable or uncaused, great art was usually produced in fairly predictable situations. For example, very often great artists had had fathers or even grandfathers who happened to be artists; in other words, often it was a family endeavor. Naturally, someone who's interested in art is going to encourage progeny in that direction. And I found many father-son or even grandfather-father-son art situations. Second of all, I found that if the talented child in question happened to be a woman the chances of her going on to be what is considered a "genius," that is, an innovator in the field of art, were minimal no matter what degree of early talent she showed. For example, going to the museum in Barcelona and looking at the early work of Picasso is really an eye-opener. He was a very, very talented little boy and his early work is extraordinary—he was indeed a child prodigy. I might also point out that his father was an artist and a teacher of art. I asked myself: what if Pablo had been Pablita? What if he had been a girl? I went to the Brooklyn Museum class for talented children and there really were girls in that class who were also little *wunderkinder*—little child prodigies—who did work on the level of that of the twelve-year-old Picasso. What happened to them? Why didn't their genius come to fruition in the way that Picasso's did? One tends to think that in any situation innate genius will come out no matter what the odds are against it. But it does not come out, no matter what the odds are against it. It comes out only in very special circumstances, and it fails to fulfill its potential in very definable circumstances too; and one of those circumstances of almost guaranteed failure is if the child prodigy in question happens to be a woman. There are no doubt many unsung Pablita Picassos who are doing dish washing or being sales girls simply because of the fact that they are women.

Now this of course forced me to raise other issues in art. Feminism not only asks questions about the position of women in society, it seems to me that it forces basic ideological questioning of many other assumptions we accept as normal in a given culture or a given society. In other words, if you ask why are there so few women who have pursued successful careers or are what we call geniuses in the fine arts, feminism forces us to be conscious of other questions about our so-called natural assumptions. That is one way in which feminism affects cultural institutions: it sets off a chain reaction. From your feelings about injustice or your feelings about wanting to push further into issues like that of genius you could go on to question a great many other assumptions that govern the discipline as a whole and ask why art history has focussed so exclusively on certain individuals and not others, why on individuals and not on groups, why on art works in the foreground and something called social conditions in the background rather than seeing them as mutually interactive. In other words, you can question the entire paraphernalia and standards of the discipline or institution that you're working in.

In addition, my involvement in feminism has led me to question some of the standards and values by which we have judged art in the past. In the article I wrote, "Why Have There Been No Great Women Artists?," I said that I thought that simply looking into women artists of the past would not really change our estimation of their value. Nevertheless, I went on to look into some women artists of the past and I find that my estimations and values have in fact changed. Another plus to feminism which I think can make one more flexible, more open to abandoning or rejecting our own previous positions when we find that we're wrong. I think that's another thing that I've learned from the feminist movement: not to stick to a position because one's ego is involved in it but to let go of an old idea and see how a new one works. In any case, I have been looking into women artists of the past and I find that in the process of examining them my whole notion of what art is all about is gradually changing.

For example, one of the artists in the past that I had always been taught to look down on as a horrid example of the salon machine manufacturer *par excellence* was Rosa Bonheur, a laughing stock, the prototypical academic painter. Now I've gotten very interested in Rosa Bonheur. First of all it's interesting to know that she was the most popular painter in the United States. She was probably the only painter who was really known out in the Middle West or in the Far West, by means of prints and reproductions. She was practically the only painter that a lot of people were acquainted with and I still know older women who say they grew up in Kansas or upper New York State and the only art work they had was a print of *The Horse Fair* that hung in the kitchen. That was their contact with art—Rosa Bonheur. And I asked myself why has she been rejected? It's not because she's a woman. I'm not naive enough to think that that is the reason: it's because the style of art that she made went out of fashion.

But being interested in realism and being interested in a kind of justice for art—rejected styles need some support and some help just as rejected people do!—I decided to look into the work of Rosa Bonheur and I came up with interesting results. The results were so interesting that I decided to look into other nineteenth century women artists as well and have done further work on Rosa Bonheur. It is certainly significant to Rosa Bonheur's development as an artist that her father had been an active member of the utopian Saint-Simonian community at Menilmontaut. The Saint-Simonians were firm believers in equality for women. They disapproved of marriage; they believed in equal educational opportunity; they advocated a similar trousered costume for both sexes; and they made strenuous efforts to find a woman messiah to share their leader's reign. All of this must have made an enormously strong impression on the young Rosa Bonheur whose father was himself an artist, although a struggling one, supporting the point that art tends to run in families. (Another interesting fact derived from research on Rosa Bonheur was that the Saint-Simonians were among the first to believe in total mutual dependency. Their garments all buttoned in the back which meant that you had to get a fellow member of the community to button you—a very interesting symbolic idea.)

The notion of egalitarianism for women must have made a profound impression on the young Rosa Bonheur. "Why shouldn't I be proud to be a woman?" she once responded to an interviewer. "My father, that enthusiastic apostle of humanity, many times reiterated to me that woman's mission was to elevate the human race, that she was the messiah of future centuries. It is to his doctrines that I owe the great and noble ambition which I have conceived for the sex which I proudly affirm to be mine and whose independence I will support to my dying day." *The Horse Fair* is indeed a work of noble ambition. There is nothing stereotypically feminine, i.e., soft, delicate or dainty, in this powerful, highly charged work. Its overpowering size itself constitutes a self-confident answer to the challenge of the young woman artist's abilities. The theme of human strength pitted against animal energy depicted in *The Horse Fair* had existed as far back as classical antiquity: indeed Rosa Bonheur claimed that she received her initial inspiration for the painting when she went, as she often did, to study horses from life, wearing masculine costume, at the Parisian horse market, where the sight of the horse dealers showing off their merchandise suddenly reminded her of the Parthenon frieze. So there she was, dressed like a man, full of vigor, watching the men show off their wonderful Percheron horses. (And I might add that *The Horse Fair* started a vogue for Percherons which made the breed popular throughout this country.)

She immediately went to work setting down her initial impression. The final *Horse Fair* is based on many studies from life and preliminary sketches. But it is a work in which the raw material of immediate observation has been transformed in the interest of more

The *Horse Fair* by Rosa Bonheur. Courtesy: The Metropolitan Museum of Art. Gift of Cornelius Vanderbilt, 1887.

lasting values. Forms have been generalized and idealized to emphasize the muscular vitality of the animals. The surge of movement is heightened by skillful manipulation of the dynamics of the composition. Adrienne Rich in a recent issue of *MS* magazine commented on the stifling of women's energies and the resulting vague sorrow, melancholia and despair characteristic of women's poetry in the nineteenth century. When we look at *The Horse Fair* how refreshing it is to find an artistic statement in which a woman's energy, all her vigor and power, far from being stifled, find a direct equivalent in the grandeur and dynamism of the work itself. For the real subject of *The Horse Fair* is energy, physical freedom and power: energy as displayed by a woman and the pride and joy that both humans and animals take in the visible demonstration of energy. While many modern critics have disparaged Bonheur's masterpiece as a typical salon *machine* of its time—for instance John Rewald, an authority on the art of the nineteenth century, recently characterized *The Horse Fair* as "highly expendable" and a "majestic exercise in futile dexterity"—it is well to remember that present-day judgments of nineteenth century art are themselves in the process of reevaluation. Many of the works cast aside earlier in the twentieth century as salon machines or kitsch are now being reconsidered in contexts less exclusively determined by formalism and the emphasis on "pure" pictorial qualities.

In the light of this reevaluation it is again worthwhile to look back at the positive judgments of the paintings by Bonheur's contemporaries, like the reviewer in the *British Art Journal* who wrote about *The Horse Fair* in 1857, "There is a freshness in this picture and a living power and a deep yet simple sympathy with nature which causes it to grow upon the spectator and make one wish to look on it again and again." Here, then, is an instance of how a feminist approach may bring about reevaluation, making us look again at pictures which have been cast aside and really rethink of the implications of this rejection, making us ask what elements exist within the work of art that one might look at from a feminist viewpoint.

Still another area in art history that I have been examining is that of nineteenth century Britain. It surprised me to find out that approximately 3000 names of women artists were listed in Grave's catalogue of artists who exhibited in London during the nineteenth century. A lot of them it's true showed one flower painting in one minor show, but many of them showed consistently in the most prestigious showplace of all—The Royal Academy. How many people can call to mind a single nineteenth-century British woman painter? It is hard. These women, 3000 strong, have been simply dropped from the rolls of history. Since art history demands detective work and a desire to track down historical facts, I wanted to find out who these women were and what had happened to them. And I did find quite an interesting group of artists for a big exhibition of women painters which will take place at the Los Angeles County Museum in 1976 or '77. This exhibition is itself an example of how feminism can affect our cultural institutions, because such a large scale show of women artists at a major museum would, I think, have been unthinkable ten years ago. This is an example of how feminist pressure, women's interest in the arts, and the work of feminist groups, in Los Angeles particularly, have assured the fact that women are finally going to reappear in art history.

Some of the most interesting nineteenth-century British women painters are those who did narrative painting, painting which tells a story, which is generally realist in character and which follows in the great British tradition established by Hogarth and carried on throughout the nineteenth century. Narrative painting has been singularly neglected and rejected for a variety of reasons (having nothing to do with the issue of women artists) by critics and art historians of today. Through my study of these nineteenth-century women painters, my admiration for and my interest in the whole realm of narrative and genre painting has risen enormously. And I began to ask myself why it is that traditional art history has taught us to admire, respect and devote our lives to the difficult and complex iconography of Van Eyck or Dürer or Michelangelo with its erudite religious references, its neo-platonic double meanings, its hidden references to contemporary events, and has simply cast aside or laughed at the equally rich, meaningful and in many ways complex

The Water Quilt (detail). Photo: Eberhard Otto.

iconography of this narrative genre painting of the nineteenth century. Why is this content, often dealing with social issues in the lives of ordinary men and women and with the moral problems of the day, cast aside as trivial whereas what seems to me rather paltry and silly questions about neo-platonic doctrine in the sixteenth century is taken enormously seriously, suitable for a lifetime of scholarly work? Why is there this kind of value dichotomy governing our cultural institutions? Here again feminism led me to ask questions which are not necessarily totally concerned with the issue of women. Feminism is like a key that unlocks many of the closed compartments in the mind, compartments created by one's "natural" expectations which now have to be revised, cast aside, sorted out again.

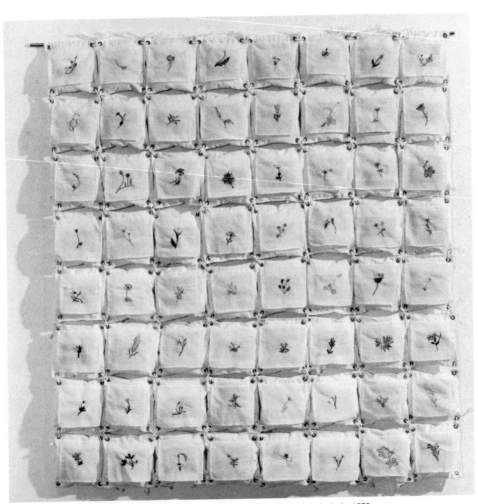

The Water Quilt by Joyce Weiland (Canada), embroidered cotton and printed cloth, 1970.
Collection: The Art Gallery of Winnipeg. Courtesy: *artcanada*. Photo: Eberhard Otto.

Rose Gonzalez and two of her award-winning pots (Pueblo, N.M.). Courtesy: Exxon Company, U.S.A.

Still another issue raised by the examination of nineteenth-century women artists is that of the democratization of the very *creation* of art. I have been looking more seriously at decorative art since my involvement in the women's movement, for the decorative arts are one of the realms in which women were "permitted" to express themselves in the past. In the course of investigating the work of American women artists of the nineteenth century, especially those of the Peale family, I found out that there were a whole group of what are known as "theorem" painters: women painters who painted from patterns or stencils; these were the ancestors of our paint-by-dot kits. There were in fact rule books and stencils— ("theorem" meant stencil)—so that women could make their own works of art by using stencils, following directions about what colors to apply, using sample patterns and so on. According to one authority in the field in nineteenth-century America women turned away from more elaborate types of embroidery, lacemaking, and stitchery because they simply did not have time to do it in the New World. They wanted an easier, quicker means of self-expression: theorem painting was one way of doing it.

In a certain sense, then the democratization of art-making took place in the United States in the hands of women. One may or may not think this is a good thing: the issues of "creativity" or "individual expression" raised by such procedures are far from clear. Perhaps painting from stencils was a kind of conceptual art before its time. It raises all sorts of interesting issues but it is not so far away from the intention behind what Seurat and the Neo-Impressionists were to do later on in France. Seurat and his friends, Signac, Cross and the others, were ardent practising anarchists who really believed in the democratization of art. They believed in painting subjects from everyday life, in painting working-class suburbs: the *Island of La Grande Jatte* has to do precisely with ordinary and upper-class people mixing in a working-class outing place. And Seurat and his friends also tried to invent a system whereby the making of art could be universally available to all. His friend, Charles Henry, invented something called the aesthetic protractor which was a method of judging lines and colors suitable to the mood and subject you wanted to express. Seurat codified his system, saying that lines above the horizon created a gay mood, lines below the horizon a sad mood, emphasize blue and purple dots for an evening calm painting. This was a way of making pictorial expression more generally available. He also boasted that he could work on *La Grande Jatte* by gaslight, for his "system" worked so perfectly that he knew exactly how many dots of which color he could apply to each area in order to produce a given effect, no matter what the lighting condition might be.

This does have democratizing implications. We may now object to Seurat's system as being a mechanization of art, a kind of dehumanization of it. But to Seurat and to many of the people around him, as well as to these women theorem painters, this was not the issue. The point was that more people could derive the satisfaction of creating something for themselves that they thought of as art, no matter what our particular present-day judgments of it are. And we have to remember, too, that the whole notion of the standardized, the mechanical, and the repeatable did not necessarily have the negative implications at that time that it has now. Mechanization and standardization were seen as instruments of democracy, ways of making more and more available to more and more people, not as instruments of alienation or dehumanization. Here again my interest in the women's movement forced me to rethink certain issues and certain innovations in the field of nineteenth-century art which I hadn't really thought about before.

These then are some of the ways in which "we as individuals and members of social groups can effect change." That is, by doing, writing, publishing, spreading, and simply thinking about issues in our own fields. I don't believe one can separate thought and action: I think thought is action. I don't believe that going out and waving a muscle means that you're acting. I believe thinking is one of the most important forms of action because it's the form of action that leads you to truth and it is only through truth that you can arrive at what is really the whole point of the women's movement and that is the implementation of justice. If we don't know what is true, it seems to me we cannot implement what is just, and for me, justice is the main goal of the women's movement, not all women

loving each other, or women establishing a realm of special virtue (because I don't think that women are especially virtuous nor need they be). But I think that our first priority is to implement justice.

By that I mean two different things: primary justice or the abolition of primary prejudice but even more important, the abolition and combating of secondary injustice or discrimination. And let me differentiate. By primary injustice I mean the very obvious fact that there are no women in the Supreme Court, that there are almost no women bank presidents—maybe there's one —that there's never been a woman president of the United States, that it is very hard even in the realm of the arts to mention a woman museum director. But in any case those are the obvious and visible manifestations of injustice. Women are simply openly deprived of visible opportunity. On that, we work with affirmative action, we work on making sure that faculties at colleges and universities are as co-educational as the student bodies. (Why is it that we call a college "co-educational" when it has a half male, half female student body, but not half men and half women faculty?) The area of overt discrimination—primary injustice—is our first fight, but it's not really the major fight.

The major fight is against secondary injustices. And by secondary injustice I mean the whole way that women are dealt with from the moment they enter the world. I mean the fact that men very often show more attention to, are rougher with and more demanding with their male children than with their female children. I mean what a child entering a nursery school sees and experiences. All the teachers there are women. In other words, right away male and female children are indoctrinated with the notion that women are there to serve their needs while men are off doing something else, presumably more important.

I would also question the notion that "boys will be boys"—in other words, permission and encouragement for roughness, brutality, violence, ignoring the sensibilities of others granted to young people of one sex: male; reproval (and kids get the notion very quickly of what is approved and disapproved) either voiced or not of such behavior in women. I don't have to mention too many examples. Another might just be the assumption that it is women's duty to arrange for child care and the management of the house, even if she does have a job, that she's the one automatically that is supposed to assume that burden. Would one dare ask a busy executive to worry about the babysitters, the meal planning and household trivia? But women who are the equivalent of busy executives or who work all day in supermarkets standing on their feet are constantly asked to assume these responsibilities which in a just society would be taken care in more positive ways by day care, by living arrangements in which some of these services are built in, or by actual sharing; and it seems to me that until this secondary discrimination is done away with, until truly we have created an androgynous society, a society where it doesn't matter what kind of sexual organs you have but you do what you are fitted for, dividing the burdens half and half or taking turns—until we have that, we still have injustice. I think that it is the business of the feminist movement in every field and on every level to combat both of these types of injustices, through action, through thought, through the pursuit of truth, and through the constant questioning and piercing through of our so-called "natural" assumptions. And it's only in this way that feminism can be a real weapon for justice for 51 percent of humanity, which is us. ☐

DEVELOPING CAREERS IN THE ARTS

Discussion Leader: Doris Freedman
President, City Walls, Inc., New York

Doris Freedman: Artists throughout history have had periods where they have come out and made strong social statements and involved themselves in broader communities. But traditionally they have worked in the isolation and privacy of their own creation. This is changing now and because it is new careers in the arts are developing— particularly for women.

Arts councils and street theatre groups are two cases in point. In almost every case that I'm familiar with the spirit behind these organizations is a woman. While the administrative positions in these groups started out as voluntary positions, today all the councils have paid executive directors.

Clare Spark-Loeb: When you have a woman in an administrative position on a newspaper, television or radio station, things begin to happen. I devoted many hours of radio programming to a group of women called the Feminist Theater. They told me the group involved around thirty women who did their own research, writing, directing, technology—everything. These women built new careers for themselves. A woman who had been an actress became a director and the success of this experience opened her eyes and gave her new confidence. Career aspirations were raised incredibly. And I cannot urge women strongly enough to get into journalism and every aspect of communications. If a woman is not around to cover stories then these things don't happen in the community. Without reporting of events accurately the people don't know about them. People remain invisible to themselves—they don't validate their own experience.

Unfortunately, people don't tend to believe their experience unless they see it validated by media, which is a different issue, but I think the opportunities in alternative media, for instance, are absolutely extraordinary. Having a free press can change power relationships within a city simply because secrecy is out and people know what's going on. Artists and creative people can speak directly to the public without the mediation of whatever special interest group is interested in keeping those opinions out of the public focus. Please don't ignore the need to get into the mass media.

Grace Glueck: One of the problems that we have at *The New York Times* is that there are very few women in administrative positions in journalism. It's an impossible situation. I think *The New York Times* has three women editors who have really, essentially, not a great deal of power. Newspapers have no licenses—you cannot challenge them in that way. I think one of the ways in which they have to be challenged is from their audience. I think that women ought to make it their business to write to newspapers, to really bombard them. I wish that people would write to *The New York Times* and say, "Why do you not have any women executives on your masthead?"

Vera Mowry Roberts: When you open any magazine or any newspaper, look at the editorial board and if the women are down there with the secretaries, write them and ask what goes on.

Perry Miller Adato: Right now in terms of developing careers in the arts one of the most immediately available ways for women to express themselves as people, as women, and as feminists, is to learn the videotape technique. The machinery is not that difficult to learn. Friends of mine who had never handled it were experts within a couple of months and have developed careers. Specifically, there is a New York group which was originally called Women Make Movies and is now called the Chelsea Picture Center. They have got one video-tape cartridge camera and sound equipment to go with it. These women are secretaries, housewives, teachers, teenagers—many without any experience. Anyone who wants to make a film or videotape can get training, assistance, and borrow the equipment. They have made dramatic movies and documentaries. Often they have organized from the neighborhood. Actors, directors, cameramen—they are all amateurs and women. Some of the work is extremely interesting. For example, three of the films deal with rape and fear. The tapes are made available to community groups and they are shown in churches and in schools.

A number of the women have begun to work in this medium on a part-time basis. I don't think that they will necessarily become professional but there are open channels—cable television is a good example. One of the first things we have to do as far as new careers for women is concerned is to use pressure to get these channels open to public groups and organize ourselves to make products that we can force these channels to show.

Lorraine Gross: We are talking about work that eventually leads to a lifelong rewarding kind of career. I don't envision the chance to show these programs on a locked-in channel on television as leading to a real career, other than as a training ground.

Lee Weiss: We seem to be only talking about New York City where all kinds of facilities are available. I think the one thing that an artist anywhere can do is to flood the local newspapers with news stories about art accomplishments, about volunteer projects that they are doing, etc. Instead of having just one or two little organizations submitting materials about what that organization is doing, every practicing artist should be telling as many people as possible about what is going on. Many of us do show in Washington and in New York and in Chicago. We should let the local people know that women are doing this and it has nothing to do with seeking publicity—it has to do with spreading the word. You give them some pragmatic suggestions, you submit articles to magazines, you do public speaking for the library. You raise the consciousness of the whole community. It just takes a little bit of gutwork.

Doris Freedman: It is most important to find out what financial and supportive resources are available in your communities. Is there a possibility of obtaining grant money? Are there existing groups in community centers, churches, schools, or other structures who could back you? For example, there was a leader in the Bronx, Irma Flack, who not only did a cultural survey of her community but who was also very politically astute. When she formed her arts council, she involved not only artists and businessmen who could provide some funding but also involved politicians. Quite often the borough president was on her board; councilmen, assemblymen and the state senator served as advisors. This is very important for us in the arts if we really are aiming towards social change. We have to bring in every element of our society including the establishment which we are reacting against.

Patricia Burnett: May I tell you about a positive action that has been taking place in Detroit? This action challenges the media. We used to just gently ask to be let in, but the hell with that. You have to make them let you in and there are ways to do it. NOW formed a caucus and we went to work with other groups to make a power block. We joined with black groups, the NAACP, the welfare mothers, WHEEL, and League of Women Voters, and we said the media is rotten toward women so let's challenge their licenses. We tackled the three television stations in Detroit and really brought them to their knees. And we made a landmark settlement with them, but it took a lot of really gutsy work.

We had three women working from eight in the morning until midnight in an office. They each worked four hours; one watched the programs, one watched the commercials, and one watched the other two. We made sure that nobody fell asleep. You've got to have five hundred hours of listed time to show that you know exactly what the stations are doing. The results were totally shocking—thirty soap operas and the rotten way they depicted women. Nothing was said about any women's activities and so forth. Anyway the stations got very scared and Channel 7 had a New York lawyer fly in four times to meet with us. We were prepared. We got in touch with Sylvia Roberts, who by the way instituted a suit against Bell Telephone and won forty-three million dollars worth of back pay for the women employees of Bell. And, as a result of our action, one station finally had to hire thirty new women. In addition we are sending in a consciousness-raising group once every two weeks to talk to every single person who works in that office to tell them what they are doing wrong and what women want, and we are getting a half-hour weekly program for women. Right now the other two channels are going to sign with us because they don't want to be sued.

Scene from "TV," one of three plays comprising *America Hurrah* by Jean-Claude van Itallie.
Producer: Stephanie Sills (New York).

If you send away to the national office of NOW in Chicago, we will send you a booklet for $2.50 on how to challenge your television stations. The whole procedure is written up. You need a feminist lawyer in your town but she doesn't have to do much because you will be prepared. The booklet even tells you the technique for handling a busy executive who wants to shut you up. The minute he says, "Well, you ladies, how about a half-hour show on this Sunday? Will that make you happy?"; you say, "We want it once a week and we want a half-hour of prime time."

Adolph Suppan: I was going to ask if a converted feminist can have about two or three minutes. I would like to talk about the seizure of power. I will use the university administrative structure as an example although I think that the parallels for that administrative structure are present in private corporations and institutions of every kind.

I am the Dean of Fine Arts at the University of Wisconsin-Milwaukee, and I belong to an organization which is called the International Council of Fine Arts Deans. At last count there were about eighty-five fine arts deans that belonged to this organization and there was only one women dean in the arts. I am going to start with that fact and then I am going to talk about the seizure of power.

Out of eighty-five fine arts schools there is one woman dean. Unfortunately, this issue really has nothing to do with affirmative action because affirmative action can't be effective because of the way university power is structured. And here is what happens. In many universities when you have an opening for an administrative position the president or chancellor creates a search and screen committee. How many women are there on such a search and screen committee? Not many. Now you have to get women on these committees and you've got to demand it and sue them if they don't. There are dozens of search and screen committees created in the large universities every year with very few women on them. What do these committees do? They send out a wonderful letter saying that they are open-minded, tolerant, and they will take anyone, even women. But those are just

words. That is just something that goes out mimeographed to all of the professional organizations in the country. Again, the affirmative action is just a mimeographed letter. The point is that women's organizations should approach, with belligerence if necessary, these national professional organizations and say that when the search and screen committee of the universities and colleges ask the national professional organizations for names, names of women should be given. Through this entire line of power, affirmative action plays no real part. It plays no part in the search and screen committees, and it plays no part in the national professional organizations.

Perry Miller Adato: Who are these national organizations? Is there a committee? Who sees these recommendations?

Adolph Suppan: They are sent by the chairman of the search and screen committee to the president of the national organization. I'm sure there are exceptions but very few. The point I'm making is that the powerful women's organizations which have now developed should write very strong letters. Get the full lists of national professional organizations. Find out what recommendations are being sent to hundreds of universities looking for new administrators. Because the seizure of power starts not only at the bottom but also at the top. This is one way that many of you have missed out. All the legal conventional channels of affirmative action have no place in this up and down structure.

Perry Miller Adato: I think that if anything is going to happen in the future, it does depend on powerful women's organizations. All of us have to recognize that we have to join, that we have to be active, that we have to help build powerful women's organizations which will be ready at a moment's notice to join any relevant action. Where a national organization does not have a powerful women's organization, we have to help create it because everything we are talking about here depends on that.

Clare Spark-Loeb: One of the great problems among women has been the fear of developing visible leadership. Unless we develop consistent visible leadership, we will not get elected to public office and until we get into Washington where the money gets handed out, we are not going to be there to help determine who gets it. The question of leadership has to be dealt with in each individual case. Is the leader responsive to the needs of the organization or does she see herself as autonomous?

Vera Mowry Roberts: I have just completed a thirty-five thousand mile trek across the United States and I want to tell you that there are more exciting things going on in these United States than you could think of in twenty-four days. One of the most exciting things that is happening is at the elementary school level. For example, one program called Project Impact was started in five cities two years ago. Here is a program pulling the arts together and making art central to education in the elementary schools. All of the learning that goes on in the schools grows out of the arts. It takes a very special kind of person to be able to handle this and the people I have met at this conference are exactly the kind of people who ought to be mixed up in this.

One of the places I visited was the Conway Middle School in Philadelphia, a middle school with grades five, six, seven, and eight, in a lower-middle class neighborhood where they had an attendance rate of something like fifty percent before they started this program. After the new curriculum came into effect the attendance record on the part of the students has been ninety-five percent over the last two years. Reading levels for students coming into the school were at least three grades below the standard reading level and by the time they left they were reading at the normal level or above. Here is a marvelous new career for people.

Lee Weiss: It's the kind of career that can be shared by people who have other careers. You can have classes come to your studio. I take about one or two schools a year and break them up into groups of twenty. Have them come to your studio, get them enthused, show them your equipment, show them how you think and feel about things.

Doris Freedman: There is a similar program where practicing artists go and work in the schools. Writers were perhaps the first to start this kind of program with their Teach-

ers and Writers Collaborative. Poets and writers are sent directly to the schools for a period of time to expose young people to a new way of approaching English, their own thinking, and their language. I was very privileged once to walk with Kenneth Koch, the poet, into a Lower Manhattan public school room filled with forty-three kids, age fourteen. Kenneth was about to give a weekly session in that class. When he walked in, the whole place became electrified. The session was magic. Now, this is important for the teacher too.

I saw the same thing happen with a sculptor, a man named Clement Meadmore. We were placing a piece of his artwork (a huge abstract semi-circular piece called Split Rain) on a public school ground and we felt that it ought not to be just plunked there. Before it even got there, the artist himself met with those kids. He didn't fit their stereotype of a funny little man with a beret who sculpts; he's a big, burly Australian sculptor who works with huge materials. And he talked to the kids about what he does and how he does it. That piece is now in the heart of graffitiland in New York City, the Inwood Marble Hill section of Washington Heights. You can't see a block that isn't written over, but his piece is clean. If someone marks it, the students come out and wash it off.

Vera Mowry Roberts: I'm one for thinking of practical things to do. If you are interested in discovering about the artists in the school program, send to the U.S. Office of Education for a book called *Artists in the Schools*. If you are interested in the Project Impact program, ask for the report on that.

Doris Freedman: There is also a group called Affiliate Artists, a New York based outfit, which sends artists all over the country.

Vera Mowry Roberts: There is another group called Alliance for the Arts in Education and I would advise all of you to keep your eye on it and get yourselves mixed up in it. This is an alliance between state departments of education, state arts councils, and representatives of the professional societies in theatre, music, dance, and art, and any other interested citizens. These people are being charged with developing all of the

Magic Tree by Marjorie Kreilick (Madison, Wis.), marble mosaic.

arts, by any means possible, within state boundaries. You can find who your state chairman is by writing to the superintendent of public instruction in your state because he's charged with getting the thing set together. The staff person in New York is Forbes Rogers at the Kennedy Center. He would also be helpful in giving you information. It is in the formative stage and it needs input from everybody.

Doris Freedman: Can I just throw out one more piece of information to those of you who are starting to challenge institutions? There is a group called Volunteer Lawyers in the Arts and it is very important for groups who don't have the resources when they are initially starting out. There is a base in New York and it is worthwhile to write to them because they are nationalized. □

HIGHER EDUCATION AND WOMEN

Discussion Leader: Margaret Mahoney
Vice President, Robert Wood Johnson Foundation, Princeton, New Jersey.

Margaret Mahoney: I would like to propose that we use this session to get down on paper and in our own heads how to manipulate the system to get what we all really want. If we're going to define a program and try to get it going, we must first get a definition of the conflict and of the resolution of the conflict.

Patricia Kerr Ross: Higher education is charged with placing young people (half of which are women) into professional roles. There are two aspects of this problem. First, more women should be placed in positions of responsibility within institutions of higher education. And second, the institutions of higher education themselves should help place their women students in places of responsibility in other institutions.

Athena Tacha Spear: I think that the role of higher education and the responsibility toward women students is not only to advise them how to find careers but to train them to be able to pursue a career and be willing to fight to get it, because obviously you can't find positions for them.

Nancy Knaak: I think one of our most difficult problems is to help the young woman student who enters as a freshman to raise her level of aspiration when she has already had eighteen years of being told to compromise. We must help young women do more than to take second best in life.

May Stevens: The disciplines themselves should be more accurate about women.

Margaret Mahoney: That will be one of your solutions.

Ann Snitau: Which brings up another question, a strategic question: Do we want a separate women's studies program in our institutions of higher learning or do we in fact want to start putting pressure on all the departments of the university? If you don't have a women's studies program, you can't get money—you don't have an office or power base. On the other hand, if you become a separate new college often the rest of the university feels that they have paid their dues and the effort ends there.

Ravenna Helson: What about reducing institutional rigidities in higher education, such as the terrible difficulty of half-time appointments or the nepotism rules that at the present time anyway work against women?

Margaret Mahoney: Are there other problems that are serious. Financial aids for women?

Ravenna Helson: That and child care.

Athena Tacha Spear: My feeling about day care centers is that whenever they exist, which is rare, they are a sort of favor to women who work. We have to change that attitude. If there are no day care centers and the mother wants to work or study, her husband must understand that he has an equal responsibility for child care and cooking and dishes and so on. It is not de facto a woman's responsibility.

Margaret Mahoney: This is a good example of getting to the solution without studying the problem. One solution is day care centers but the problem really is proper care of children which insures that the freedom of neither parent is impaired.

Lorraine Gross: There is another question that has been bothering me a great deal. I work mostly with men in the university and I find that my ideas are sort of pooh-poohed—they're saying in effect you're a frivolous female type. How can we as women change our way of talking or how can we become more effective?

Faith Ringgold: The politicians involved with Watergate probably had unfrivolous, very clear-cut thoughts about things and they created very big problems. I don't think that men today are succeeding very well in the ways their minds work and I don't think that it is going to be of benefit to emulate them in doing that. I don't think that their institutions are working and I don' think that their society is working. In fact, I know that it is not. What women are doing is maybe a little crazy and chaotic but the most important thing that is happening in this world is that women are speaking up.

Margaret Rahill: Nonetheless, we need people who know how to negotiate, who know how to be tough as well as tactful and to know our grounds.

Nathan Feinsinger: Everybody should have, even in higher education, some concept of negotiation. There is a distinction, first of all, between negotiation, which is a face-to-face discussion by the principals concerned, and a discussion where we have intervention by third parties in one form or another—mediators, fact-finders, arbitrators. What is needed at the university level is to have available third parties with no direct interest in the dispute, whose sole function is to help in settlement and, most important, they must be completely independent. Now that is the problem. If you are talking about picking someone from within the ranks of

the university, he or she belongs to somebody. The chancellor usually appoints them.

Margaret Mahoney: Is this the problem with affirmative action?

Nathan Feinsinger: Yes, the affirmative action person is usually the chancellor's assistant. The question is how can you get justice when the supposed impartial person is appointed by the opposition?

Pat Clark: Would you suggest that women who have a particular case in the university against affirmative action hire a lawyer?

Nathan Feinsinger: No. There should be a so-called grievance and arbitration procedure established by agreement between the parties. A panel of say half a dozen people in which both sides have confidence. And that is easily done. The question is: Will both sides be willing to give that third party the power of decision? I don't think that most administrations would do that.

Nancy Knaak: It may work with some of the secondary schools. We have all the grievance procedures but usually we can act only in an advisory capacity. A chancellor can always refuse a recommendation.

Margaret Mahoney: How do you get beyond the advisory point?

Nathan Feinsinger: Many campuses where the administration (which is the management) would normally not agree to arbitration see that the union is coming out of the pipes. And they know that the first thing the unions are going to demand is an agreement by arbitration procedure, and if they can set up an arbitration procedure before the union does, most people would say that they don't need a union.

Ann Snitau: I want your opinion on whether or not the grievance procedure would create a diffusing of the possibilities of unionization.

Nathan Feinsinger: You take what you can while you can get it.

Faith Ringgold: To have the power of the elite, it would require that people be very articulate and that those articulate people be good people and that may not be the same thing. I think that unions are also corrupting.

Nathan Feinsinger: I think that the problem of women in higher education would eventually be resolved by collective bargaining through the union. It may be five years, it may be ten years, but it's coming.

Ravenna Helson: I would like to bring up a related question: Would we want to say anything about always encouraging the departments that are most technological, the most male, and abolish the decorative arts departments? Do we want to take a stand on that?

Pat Clark: I had some friends in California who no longer have any tenure in the arts department in the California system.

Ravenna Helson: Now this is sort of the same kind of decision that the chancellor makes and I don't know if it is the sort of decision that would ever be subject to an arbitrator or mediator.

Nathan Feinsinger: We should first give consideration to the establishment of a grievance and arbitration procedure within the institutions. The very existence of that machinery is a barrier against injustice in many cases, because if the departmental head knows there is an avenue for voicing complaints he will think twice before he cuts off that person's head.

Margaret Mahoney: Perhaps the American Arbitration Association would be helpful in establishing this kind of procedure.

Athena Tacha Spear: One problem is how to prevent the powers in the departments—deans, chairmen—from getting rid of women by not giving them tenure. But the major problem is how to get in more women and for this you need separate legislation which will force them to hire a higher percentage of women faculty.

Nancy Knaak: They are already required to do this by law.

Athena Tacha Spear: Yes, but we want internal legislation—a commitment that within the next five years they'll reach a certain percentage of women faculty.

Margaret Mahoney: Isn't the research assistant route one way to get more women on the faculty? In other words, to get more posts for women you have to get them not just in the system of education and advance training, but into job roles within the institutions.

The other issue of how do you get to be really effective in negotiations at any level, human and organizational, still needs to be answered. From my own experience I would say that self awareness is where you have to start and if you don't have a strong self image, which many of us do not have, get it first because you are not going to be able to relate to other women without it. This is the problem for women—relating to other women, supporting other women, communicating with other women, and then being able to communicate with the world at large. There are mechanisms for doing this—they are not group encounters in terms of some of the more drastic sessions that go on—but there are systems, such as Carl Roger's, that are refined learning experiences that most people can manage without falling apart. There are mechanisms, possibly, for bringing students together with women professors. This kind of group situation is effective.

Athena Tacha Spear: I want to say two things—first, it's not always sufficient to be a strong person and to be heard because if you're a minority the men can still pooh-pooh you. The most important thing is to fight for equal numbers. Secondly, students often want things but they don't feel strong enough to get active about it. They always fall behind in getting organized. At Oberlin it was the faculty women who organized and pushed for legislation and I think that's an effective way of doing it. We did it for the blacks, for instance. The faculty passed legislation that we will make a serious commitment to enrolling fifteen percent black students and hiring a fifteen percent black faculty within the next five years. We have reached the level of the students this year. We still haven't reached the level of the faculty. Last spring we passed the same legislation for women aiming at fifty percent. Of course, the students are always fifty percent women, but not the faculty. The faculty is now seventeen percent women, many of them untenured and many of them at the bottom, so the general faculty reluctantly made the commitment that within the next five years we will aim at a fifty percent women faculty. They also raised all the salaries of women.

Faith Ringgold: I'd like to ask you a question. When there is a group for the blacks and there is a group for women, where do I go?

Athena Tacha Spear: There are two places for you to go.

Faith Ringgold: No, it turns out that there is *no* place. Unless the women agree that

black women are indeed women. Sometimes they don't deal with that issue. They say, "Oh, we have a Black Studies Department," but in the Black Studies Department the head may be an African who believes that all women are supposed to stay home. And even if he's not African, he still may believe that. Therefore, there is literally no place for black women to go.

Athena Tacha Spear: We're looking *doubly* for black women.

Faith Ringgold: What percentage of black women are benefiting from your gains at Oberlin?

Athena Tacha Spear: I suspect in terms of students that of the fifteen percent of black

Faith Ringgold and *Mother Brown with Children*. Photo by Linda Rich (Madison, Wis.).

students, half are women. There are fewer black women faculty members, but the administration has made a point of hiring black women as assistant deans, assistant provosts, etc.

Workshop Participant: Are half of the black faculty members in 1975 going to be women?

Athena Tacha Spear: We hope so but we realize that there is a limitation to the available pool.

Workshop Participant: Yes, that's what I mean—the available pool—so what if you have nice standards. How are you going to get women to fulfill those standards once you've set them?

Margaret Mahoney: Can I ask one thing which relates back to the question of how you do it? Didn't you have to first of all get some information and concrete data so that you could move with assurance? You knew the situation in your institution and you documented it.

Athena Tacha Spear: Well, it happened that we were lucky. We have a very lively president who could push the feminist cause and he nominated an Ad Hoc Committee of Women who studied the situation and gave a lengthy report of what the situation was at Oberlin. They presented the report and recommendations of how to improve the situation to the general faculty and, fighting every bit of the way, got it passed, giving part-time employees, which are usually women, full status with tenure and all other benefits. It was a very important piece of legislation.

Margaret Rahill: It would be useful to have an outline of that procedure step by step because that's how most of these things are done.

Athena Tacha Spear: I would be glad to make it available to anyone who is interested in it.

Margaret Mahoney: I realize which problems you really think are important because we've been able to talk about some of the possible solutions and resources to solving things. The first was obviously this question of resolution of conflict, recognizing that you've got to meet conflict and how do you do it. I think that the second is how do you develop more women at different levels.

Linda Nochlin: In getting equal numbers of women, one issue is always raised that women are hired on a lower level. But I think that this is a two-sided issue because often big universities cop out on the equal numbers of women faculty issue by getting a few superstars. I know that Yale and Harvard (Harvard has hardly even put itself out that far) managed to get a few super-duper people, but on the lower levels where it's really going to count they don't bother. It is equally important to fill the lower levels because those lower levels are later on going to be the upper levels.

Margaret Mahoney: There is the problem in any field of where do you get the names of competent women. It is darn hard to know where the talent is at this very moment.

Athena Tacha Spear: The women's caucus in the College Art Association is planning to form a directory of the available pool of candidates for art history positions and art positions. It is gathering data on how many women are doing what, where they are in terms of the total picture in this country and then within single institutions.

Margaret Mahoney: A visiting program, for example, in any of the fields, but particularly in the arts would be extremely helpful for the students as well as the administration to see that there are women with talent. It's also another way of developing a pool of talent.

Lorraine Gross: With regard to visiting artists and writers in residence, there's the Affiliate Artist's program. It is an excellent program which has worked all over the United States placing women in various communities.

Faith Ringgold: I would suggest the Creative Artist's Public Service Program (CAPS). Though it is just for New York State, it's a good prototype.

Lois Jones Pierre-Noel: And the Women's Registry has a list of over five hundred women artists. □

Gerti Sennett

THE RAINBOW'S OF KEE-MAE-WON

Gently, gently, sprinkle your rain upon my Mother,

And paint a picture of many colors across

The shoulders of my Father as he passes in the sky.

Softly, softly, give drink to the flowers of my Mother,

And carry their colors, on the wings of the eagle,

Banners of ribbons across the eastern sky.

Tenderly, tenderly, your showers yield

With beauty, from your lodge of misty fires.

Kee-mae-won, send your rainfeathers from the sky.

Landscape Handbag by Eleanor Moty (Madison, Wis.), sterling silver with silver photo-electroplated image, assorted metal inlay, brass, and agate.

LAMENT OF THE SUN-DANCER

I. — The Capture

Shaman, Shaman, prepare a sacred lodge for me;
Make a bed of sage near the buffalo head altar;
Cross flowing waters and capture a Sacred Tree;
Have my uncles of the red hands paint my pole,
And place well the cedar boughs for the nativity.

II. — The Torture

Shaman, Shaman, raise the Sacred Pole high,
To spin my skewered body into a vision;
Rock me on deerskin tendons from sunsky to sunsky;
Let blood mingle with sweat to bathe me,
For my heart is strong, and my mind will never cry.

III. — The Captivity

Drummers, Drummers, beat my Sun Gaze Dance slowly and rest,
That they may count coup on my aching limbs;
Bind high the thongs, keep my feet from my Mother's breast;
Letting my aunts send songs to dwell in my ears,
And my grandmothers provide herbs for my bleeding chest.

IV. — The Escape

Shaman, Shaman, white cloud plumes cool my head;
My eyes have looked into a dream, my vision completed;
Young maidens with sweet-grasses wipe away red
Blood dripping from my wounds, soaking the lodge floor;
I have lived through my ordeal; My name is Buffalo Spits Lead.

As a Menominee Indian, Ms. Sennett added immeasurably to the conference with both the recitation of her poetry and as a spokeswoman for her people. She is currently working on the history and legends of the Menominee and a book of poetry entitled From Another Indian Summer.

KEEP YOUR HANDS ON THE PLOW: HOLD ON!

Women and the Arts Conference, Wingspread. Photo by Bob Black. Courtesy: The Johnson Foundation.

by Fannie Hicklin
*Professor of Theatre, The University
of Wisconsin-Whitewater.*

Woman's role in and with the arts was the magnet that brought together this large, diverse, articulate, inquiring group of people. There was a base of mutual agreement or understanding that the image of women has often been distorted and maligned and that women have not been able to make their potential contributions to society either qualitatively or quantitatively. This lack of realization of potential has henceforth frustrated many women and simultaneously left society diminished.

The creators of this conference—and I use the word *creators* purposefully and meaningfully—conceived the need for action in rejecting sex stereotypes and for opening broader avenues of possibilities for women. Business doors have been pounded upon; various professions have been questioned; but art as a means of social change has not been adequately explored.

The arts are the representation of man's highest aspirations. The status of health of a country, or group of people, can be directly correlated with the aesthetic concerns of that country or group. It is through the arts that it is possible to build a more creative society by humanely applying sensitivity in the use of power—in other words, affirming values and insights on which the total society can be based.

However, the arts, like women, have generally also been outside of the mainstream. First, the arts have not been associated with people at large, but rather with an elite class or a special segment of society. Second, the arts, though practiced by males and representative of their values, have, curiously enough, been deemed effeminate and therefore not good nor necessary; the arts are the frills, the periphery of our lives.

We, as women in the arts, are caught in a double bind of discrimination and myth. Therefore our challenge is to promote the arts and women simultaneously as essential forces in providing the creativity so necessary for social change and for the humane development of all people. One participant has said: "I wanted to change the world and that's why I went into the arts." Throughout this conference the qualities of compassion and understanding were stressed as the dynamic forces needed to draw us together as people: men and women of all creeds and colors. These are also qualities which as creators of art allow us to turn into ourselves with honesty and to discover our inner reality.

Recurring themes have been the need 1) to know who we are as women and how we got there; 2) to define our current place in society; and 3) to project means of getting out of the double bind in order to help implement the justice needed by all deprived peoples. We concur with the notion that the individual and the political cannot really be separated. The self is a part of society and society is an extension of the self, with interaction between the two being a constant. A responsible artist is a responsible person who uses her skills to interpret and to shape society. Shaping society necessitates action and action requires well-devised, unhackneyed strategy. Participants at this conference further aroused consciousness regarding the dilemma of women and the arts; they compared problems, they listened to divergent views. Strategies were not earth-shaking nor completed—as they shouldn't be if they are to be fresh and relevant to the diverse problems and circumstances in schools, museums, theatres, etc.

Some of the specific suggestions for immediate action are:

1. To get a common understanding of terms such as feminism, humanism, power, the arts. Linda Nochlin's interpretation of what feminism means to her was an exposition that brought understanding of the term and mutuality of feeling on the part of listeners.

2. To continue arousing consciousness in our respective demographic locations and in the various areas of the arts.

3. To avoid the destructive aggression often associated with "competing as a man" or excelling a man in order to be successful.

4. To increase the number of professional roles for women in schools and universities, museums, industries, and alternative institutions. We must establish allies in the top echelon of institutions which we wish to change. We must also get our own spokespeople in, even if tokenism seems to be the initial basis of acceptance. We must monitor. Our very presence is valuable. We can sensitize people through personal contact.

5. To encourage and promote women's studies programs.

6. To provide awareness programs on role and career definitions for undergraduate women.

7. To identify and insist on financial aids programs for women.

8. To encourage visiting women artists for lectures, programs. Black women especially desire opportunities like these for they can address themselves to both feminism and blackness.

9. To raise a new generation, with new ideas, through innovative instruction and better teachers.

10. To establish a national organization of Women in the Arts whose objective will be to promote feminism *and* the arts.

Finally, women must be highly supportive of each other. We must recognize that none of us exists in a vacuum. We influence, and we are influenced. At the same time, we must respect differences of approach to effect change. We must be tolerant; we must allow freedom of choice. We must be continuous, persistent in a steady attack on every evidence of discrimination; we must keep the faith in ourselves as creative movers. So, using words from a Negro spiritual, I charge you to "Keep your hands on the plow! *hold on!*" □

Ex-Slave With Long Memory, photo by Dorothea Lange. Courtesy: Dorothea Lange Collection, The Oakland Museum.

THE MALE ARTIST AS STEREOTYPICAL FEMALE

by June Wayne
Artist and Founder of the
Tamarind Workshop.

We artists complain about the same old problems year after year no matter how obscure or famous we may be. We ask each other how to get a show, or a better gallery, or how to move our dealers to promote our works more vigorously. We gossip a lot about the museums too: how a certain trustee collects the art of so-and-so which explains his retrospective at the Modern: or a certain balding young curator is mounting a whole exhibition to prove his pet esthetic gimmick. Every year yet another lawyer/dealer combination is said to be raiding yet another artist's estate. And obviously every issue of every art magazine proves anew how stupid critics can be.

Sooner or later one of us casually drops the word that Joseph Hirshhorn just blew into town and "bought out the studio" but no mention is made of the prices he paid—nor do we ask. We know the idiosyncrasies of all the collectors and we'd just as soon not be reminded what "making it" can mean. Artists lick their wounds for nourishment, not for healing.

Over the years I have pondered why guilds and royalties, which work fairly well for actors, writers, composers—even for scientists and inventors—never developed for visual artists too. Perhaps because we are unworldly about the practical matters of sales and careers. Neither art schools nor university art departments provide courses in business and professional problems of being an artist. A masters degree may qualify the student to replace the teacher but not to bargain with a dealer. Anyhow, who could teach such courses? Art professors cannot hack it either in the art market so new artists fare no better than preceding generations.

A union or a guild needs an industry *against which* to organize but the art scene has no single nexus of power to bargain with. As for public agencies, they break up into diffuse committees which have neither the purpose nor authority to resolve the grievances of artists. The art world lives in an ebb and flow of guerilla warfare. Such citadels of power as there are—museums, foundations, arts councils, the National Endowments—are held by *them,* not us, and only rarely can one find that an artist is a member of one of *their* committees. So we learn very early to see ourselves as esthetically unique and morally superior—which is a palatable way of saying isolated and powerless.

But neither the hostile ecology of the art milieu nor the inadequacies of art department curriculae fully explain why artists, who have as much common sense as other people, *when it comes to their art,* fail to use even the most elementary protections. For instance, why do so many artists consign their work to obviously inept or venal or fly-by-night dealers without asking so much as a receipt, let alone a contract or a credit reference? I could list many examples of idiot behavior by otherwise intelligent artists. Why does our cynicism, which is based on painful experience, only express itself in hostile passivity instead of prideful self-protection?

In recent years, the many freedom movements have sharpened my awareness of similarities between the behavior patterns of artists and other minority groupings. There is a direct relationship between the power of any oppressor and the self-esteem and self-evaluation of those who are held in check. In this context feminist literature set me thinking about the relation between women artists and sexual stereotyping. The practical utility of treating the male artist as though he were a woman struck me forcefully for it would explain much that puzzled me about the interface of artists with the rest of the art world's professionals.

It appears to me that society unconsciously perceives the artist as a female and that artists act out the feminized stereotypical patterns projected onto them. Inasmuch as these patterns are self-destructive and profoundly inhibiting to independent action, the ease with which artists are maintained in a state of disenfranchisement endures for generation after generation. It becomes profitable to many people to view the artist as one unable to cope with the real world of money and trade, although a pedestal is where the artist, like the woman, waits while others are alleged to cope in his behalf.

Although there always have been artists of both sexes, only males survived into art history. Yet even for male artists one is more apt to believe that Leonardo and Michelangelo were homosexual than that Peter Paul Rubens was a diplomat. For the ancient but still powerful demonic myth prepares us to accept the warped and bizarre personality to be an indicator of talent and even as proof of genius. Some of the characteristics that artists are given by the demonic myth are, surprisingly, almost identical with characteristics described by Betty Friedan in *The Feminine Mystique.* So profound is the stereotype of the artist as the inchoate, intuitive, emotional romantic, that both the public and the artists themselves find it difficult to imagine that we can be anything else.

The demonic myth presents the artist as one possessed of mysterious forces that well up during creative seizures as it were. The work of art is produced without the exercise of the artist's will and may even seem to be unmodified by knowledge itself. The artist "can't help it" or "doesn't know how it happened" or whence came the inspiration. Should the artist try to analyze, control, even to think peripherally about the creative moment, it may be vitiated or even destroyed. The artist is thought to be a sort of medium through whom creative miracles are manifest and unless one is BORN an artist, neither effort nor intelligence makes one into one. So the demonic myth presents the artist as biologically determined—born with Promethean fires as it were.

The feminine mystique also is based on biological determination. The woman is born to procreate and to spend her life in servicing her procreation. No effort of will or intellect is needed in order to reproduce her kind. She is a sort of medium through whom the procreative miracle is manifest. If one isn't born a woman, no effort of will or intelligence (not even surgery) can transform one into one. The biology of the woman, like that of the artist, is proposed to be her destiny.

Obviously the artist makes art and the woman makes babies, but the word *create* is

Photo by Ruth Bernhard (San Francisco).

commonly used to describe both processes. That will and brain are said to be unnecessary and even antithetical to the function of women and of artists encourages the elision of the male artist into perception as a female by the public. Semantic confusion causes operational distortion in many kinds of human experience: this is why the do-it-yourself hobbyist tells you he loves being "creative" and shows you a book shelf to prove it. Creativity, procreation and "making something" are used interchangeably in our society as though synonymous.

Lurking just below the surface of public consciousness is a pervasive assumption that any man whose feelings, intuitions and purposes are inchoate in source and unusual in product must be a homosexual. Even the most macho of male artists faces this problem and the recent tributes to Jose Limon particularly emphasized as remarkable that he brought a masculine aspect to the art of the dance. Do *real* men "go for" ballet, poetry, pictures or do they go for sports? Isn't the culture sector the province of the ladies' committees? Aren't the arts seen as girlish frills in the educational system? What papa is pleased that his son wants to be an artist? Why are art reviews published on the woman's page (between the cranberry sauce and the Simplicity patterns) in nearly every newspaper in this country?

Many kinds of authorities have insisted that womanhood is incompatible with profundity of thought, intellectual discipline or worldly accomplishment, but none puts this position more succinctly than does Helen Deutsch, Freud's eminent but submissive disciple. She writes that "Woman's intellectuality is to a large extent paid for by the loss of feminine qualities. Her intellectuality feeds on the affective life and results in its impoverishment." Change only two words and Deutsch's formulation will sound as though it had been written about artists. "The *artist's* intellectuality is to a large extent paid for by the loss of valuable *creative* qualiites. The *artist's* intellectuality feeds on the *creative* life and results in its impoverishment." A perfect fit.

That critics, art historians and even artists accept the cliche that the brain is a threat to creativity would explain why, if an exhibition is reviewed as "cerebral" or "intellectual", the words are understood as pejorative, not complimentary. There is a special limbo for Robert Motherwell who often is called the most intellectual of contemporary artists. Who envies Motherwell that niche? Not that he surely is the MOST intellectual of the artists: there are others who may be more so. But Motherwell lets himself be seen as such whereas most artists hide their mind under a bushel. Richard Diebenkorn, during a conversation with me, once called it "maintaining a low profile." Reaction to a brainy artist is like reaction to a female intellectual: neither is quite to be believed.

After I had noted the interchangeability of "artist" with "woman" I played with feminist literature, substituting artist for woman and found myriad examples where the substitution worked perfectly. (I won't take time or space to illustrate here since you can verify this easily for yourself). Next I rearranged the actors of the art milieu according to sexual roles: artists as women regardless of actual gender: dealers, collectors, curators, patrons, critics, public functionaries, et al, as men regardless of actual gender. Now the passivity of artists and the aggressiveness of these other categories became logical and predictable.

How natural that artists are inept, unworldly, insecure, gossipy, cliquish, capricious, flirtatious, indirect, devious, manipulative, over-imaginative, emotional, intuitive, unpredictable, colorful, overly aware of costume and image. Why expect artists to understand money, contracts, business? Why indeed. One must *help* artists, *support* them; they cannot cope. Accordingly we artists look for help not equality, support not self-determination. We expect "them" to take care of us, get us into the fashionable collections and make us famous. And we anxiously await results of their efforts while grousing in the studio or rapping at Barney's Beanery or on the beaches at the Hamptons in the summertime. We might as well be Lana Turner awaiting stardom at a drugstore soda counter.

Nor are our fantasies so inappropriate: what dealer does not claim to know more about nearly everything than does the artist? What curator is unsure of superior judgment of what the artist is *really* doing? What critic or reporter feels obliged to ask an *artist* what the work is all about? What collector sees the artist as anything but a freak, however lovable?

But if all this is true, why are *women* artists discriminated against? If male artists are acceptable as quasi-females in female postures, why not women artists too? Because the male artist is camouflaged by the demonic myth, not the feminine mystique. He rides motorcycles, not subways; pops drugs, not iron supplements. Groupie girls with pale sheafs of stringy hair trail after him, not his kiddies. A hundred romantic props comprise his demonic image and most are macho to the hilt. But the woman artist is only underscored to be a woman by the feminine mystique. She is an instant Mrs. So-and-so living in a tract house with hubby and the babies. She is thought to dabble in oils in the family den which only she refers to seriously as her studio. And her art is assumed to be a matter of tight little landscapes and flower arrangements or decorative, derivative abstractions displayed over the couch in an all too dreary and domestic living room. To be a wife, a mother and forty is to suffer a fatal syndrome; no matter what the truth or how large the talent or accomplishment, she is only a woman trying "to pass" as an artist.

A few of us women artists have achieved some recognition but we clearly carry demonic markings to hide our female stigmata. We live in lofts and storefronts and other wildly unconventional spaces just like the male artists do. We dress in unisex or as fantastic eccentrics. Nevelson and O'Keefe do not shop at Peck and Peck. As successful (women) artists we *must* prefer lovers to husbands and be on guard every moment against the conventionalized female gesture. If one is lesbian, so much the better: this demonizes the image and gains one the wife that every artist needs to do the scut work of a career.

For an artist's wife, whether an artist herself or not, holds the outside salaried job that pays the studio rent. She also assists within the studio, looks after the framing and shipping, writes the letters and does the phoning. She may even verbalize "his" esthetic too while HE maintains the demonic posture of not knowing what he is doing when he is creating in the studio. She plans the cocktail parties to which collectors and curators and critics are invited and she also will stand patiently aside while a female collector (that *she* fished in) exercises the male prerogative of seducing her husband. What man would do as much for an artist wife?

But all these efforts, no matter how devotedly performed, are seldom to much avail. The reality is that only a few artists at a time can be promoted in the art market as it presently functions. The art market is a secretive, unregulated, labile arena which the jargon of the Security Exchange Commission would describe as untidy. Although it is a young market insofar as contemporary American artists are concerned, already it's incestuous and even sclerotic in some respects.

When women and minority artists clamor to share the recognition and rewards available till now to a few white males, they merely add themselves into an overcrowded talent pool which art marketeers cannot serve in any case. Although no formal studies have been performed on the size and nature of the artist population some careful estimations suggest that there are something more than 300 esthetically valid artists without dealers for every artist of comparable quality with one. Furthermore, I doubt that more than one artist in fifty who do have galleries, lives from the sales the dealer generates. Every industry needs a labor reservoir from which to draw its talents but a ratio of 12% of unemployed for teachers and engineers, for example, is extremely high. Unemployment of 25 to 50% among black males under the age of 25 is the worst ratio in the nation. So you can see that 300 artists for every gallery slot is a redundancy of intolerable proportion.

Some would say there are too many artists but I believe these figures represent the underdevelopment of the market system and that the galleries serve neither the general public around the nation nor the artist population. The art dealers cluster in a few big cities where they cater to each other in alliances of ownership of particular works of art and sell these to an interchangeable clientele of moneyed urbanites. Like the two men with one diamond who sell only to each other at constantly rising prices, much of the traffic in art involves a small circle of international dealers and collectors. Since collectors have limited ability to absorb works of art (some museums have reached their limits too) sooner or later they begin to trade and their collections reenter the market to compete with newer works. So the word collector is fast becoming another word for trader—as in stocks.

Unfortunately the tax deductible structure, which was intended to encourage support for cultural institutions, can now be seen to encourage art speculators by providing downside protection against risk. Much more needs to be written about taxes, the museums, the market and the problems of artists but I only refer to them here as a frame of reference for my comment that it is profitable to some people that artists remain demonized—that is—feminized—that is, lobotomized.

The future of the art world in this country will, I believe, be profoundly influenced by the self reevaluation of women and minority artists who are reversing a previously passive acceptance of outside pressures. Many women artists note that half of nothing is nothing and to share what the male artist has been getting is to move from our harem to his. By contrast such militancy as male artists are beginning to express these days concerns itself more with the loss of teaching jobs on campuses than with changes in fundamental attitudes toward participation *as equals* in the art milieu. The shape of the art scene of the future depends on how profoundly, how philosophically, and yes, how *cerebrally,* artists come to understand themselves.

Will we reject romantic stereotypical behavior that serves to keep us down? Will we use those intellectually creative aptitudes for problem solving that we artists possess, actually, in somewhat higher measure than most other people?

Obviously if the battle for the freedom of the press and the restoration of checks and balances in the Congress are lost, artists will go down the tubes like everybody else, but if the nation makes a new commitment to freedom and life enhancement, then many options open up for artists that we did not have before. Assuming peace and freedom, by 1980 the art marketing apparatus as we know it will have enlarged somewhat but will have been largely by-passed by self-help activities by artists. The opening of studios to the public now in evidence will expand, I believe, into substantial artist-owned Cooperative Corporations comparable to the Cooperative structure used by the Canadian Government in behalf of Eskimos, and similar to the Consumer Co-ops that have a long tradition in this country. I do not mean the simplistic "share-the-rent, share-the-cleaning" cooperation we see among artists just now, but rather the professionally run, business cooperatives that have considerable tax and legal muscle within our society. Artists probably will be showing and selling through their own co-ops, and may also share housing, studio facilities, medical care, insurance and many kinds of professional services as well. I refer to P.R., accounting and legal, even catalogue and mailing services.

Everywhere artists are talking about organizing themselves one way or another. I believe the best approach will be the formation of a Guild something like the Screen Writers Guild rather than a "membership" grouping for various social action purposes. A guild with a full time professional staff could lobby out the terrible tax inequities that burden artists and ruin our families when we die. Such a guild also could lobby out (and win, I have no doubt) the right for artists to pay our income taxes with our art—as is a norm in Mexico. Such a right would then permit the government to start an art bank or library from which every sort of tax exempt institution could borrow works of art for use at community level in schools, hospitals and public buildings.

It would take such a guild to implement residual rights for artists and police the implementation of such rights and collect our royalties for us. But all this depends on whether we ourselves decide to form a guild: residual rights will not arrive as a fancy gift from the "johns" who feel they have been keeping us, like aging call girls, as an act of charity. Once artists form a power block, our guild will be able to work with other arts institutions to open up the news media to the culture sector, to provide arts news to the people and to end the blackout of creative people. The arts should have visibility comparable to that afforded sports. Perhaps in the next few years we will see the appearance of a cultural news wire service which, like AP and UPI and the Farm News Wire Service, will provide teletyped professionally written stories to all media, printed and electronic. When will arts reporters be a norm on every TV news team?

I believe that within the next few years museums will be at least partially financed by the federal government and that, as a result, there will be a forced clean-up of many of the conflicts of interest now rife within museum operations. I trust the interlocking boards of trustees will be broken up and that an artists' guild will have its representatives sitting on all museum policy making boards. But, of course, with federal money will come the increasing danger of political interference in the culture sector. It could happen that the museums, theatres, opera companies, etc. could find themselves as cannibalized by politicians as now is

happening before our very eyes to educational television.

I believe that artists must intensify discussion as to our own functions beyond the role of makers of objects as a sort of cottage industry. Art is more than product and I can see how self-determination could lead directly to the formation of a national civil service of creative people of every kind to perform those life enhancement services that reevaluation of the quality of life suggests is necessary to the survival of the species.

Freed of the hopelessness that our own banal and stereotyped behavior of the past imposed on us, both the possibilities and the problems of the future take on new and daring dimensions. I wish I had more confidence that we artists will meet the challenge. For the moment I will be content if more of us accept ourselves as the intellects we are. This first step could lead us almost anywhere—and anywhere is up from where we are. □

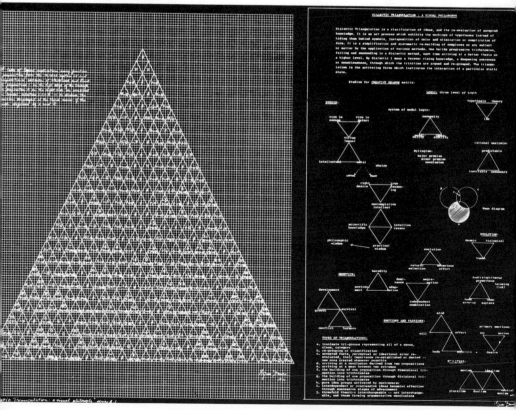

Dialectic Triangulation: A Visual Philosophy (detail) by Agnes Denes (New York), 1970.

A REEXAMINATION OF SOME ASPECTS OF THE DESIGN ARTS FROM THE PERSPECTIVE OF A WOMAN DESIGNER

We'll go that extra mile.

- We feature the cars you prefer—GM.
- We give you S & H Green Stamps.
- We offer you 1600 locations.
- We accept recognized credit cards.

Besides, we're the first in the industry to guarantee reservations through a completely computerized system. And we maintain the best conditioned fleet in the business. No wonder we grew twice as fast as our competitors last year and are now No. 2 in locations. If you're looking for someone who'll take a few extra steps to please and serve, try National.

The customer is always No. 1

NATIONAL CAR RENTAL

GREAT ADS START WITH A GREAT IDEA!

Then it's up to you — the commercial artist — to transform that idea into the reality of an effective advertisement. It takes your talent and imagination and skill to put it all together. We manufacture the tools

if a top team of educators, trainers and business executives met to develop a really results-oriented conference, they'd have...

ama's fourth annual conference on education and training

August 12-15, 1968
New York Hilton Hotel

That's a strong statement. We can make it with confidence because AMA has called on these experts to get the facts about the potential, the challenge,

and the responsibilities involved in providing a lifetime of learning for each citizen—through education and training.

First, AMA conducted extensive surveys among the registrants and panel experts who took part in previous conferences. We found out what problem areas they wanted help on ...what new educational developments they wanted covered. Then we gathered top training specialists, educators, and leaders in the "business of education"

to show you how to make the opportunities offered by education and training today the realities of tomorrow. The result is a program that will tell you about the possibilities—and problems—that education and training face in a changing society and a changing economy.

Special panels, discussion groups and "how to" sessions will examine and evaluate the uses of the new technologies - Fundamentals of Media Development and Applications

• Realistic Vocational Training - Use of Gaming and Simulation - Educational Technology on a Limited Budget

An accompanying Exhibit will show the latest developments in teaching and training equipment.

It's your stake in the future. Learn how you can help shape that future.

For a brochure including the program and a list of leaders and speakers, fill out the coupon and return it today.

Please send me more information about AMA's 4th Annual Conference on Education and Training.

Name _____

Title _____ Dept. _____

Company _____
Govt.
Ed. Inst. _____

Address _____

City _____ State _____ Zip _____

AMERICAN MANAGEMENT ASSOCIATION

The American Management Association Building
135 West 50th St., New York, N.Y. 10020
Tel. (Area Code 212) JUdson 6-8100
(TWX 212-640-5279)

"Sheer desperation made me try Cold Power" writes Mrs. Paul Schwartz, Miami, Florida

"Doubt if this is the sort of endorsement you desire, but feel it's my duty to write you anyway.

"Sheer desperation

"It wasn't the New Jersey housewives on TV that induced me to give Cold Power a try, it was sheer desperation. My whites had been getting dingier, both in hand and machine washing.

"Absolutely astounded

"I was absolutely astounded right from the start! Everything's miraculously clean. And the whites are just beautiful.

"Cannot begin to tell you what a pleasant surprise and shock this was to me. Such a joy!

"So felt I should at least confide you this brief word of thanks.

Mrs. Paul Schwartz

HEAVY DUTY COLD POWER
LAUNDRY DETERGENT
germproofs in cold water

Cold Power—gets out the worst kind of dirt in cold water. Germproofs too.

by Sheila Levrant de Bretteville
Designer, instructor in Design at the California Institute of the Arts and co-founder of the Feminist Studio Workshop at the Woman's Building, Los Angeles.

The process by which forms are made, and the forms themselves, embody values and standards of behavior which affect large numbers of people and every aspect of our lives. It is this integral relationship between individual creativity and social responsibility that draws me to the design arts. Feminism has caused me to become more self-conscious about being a woman and this awareness has become a necessary part of my creation and criticism of work in the design arts. Reading the messages of design, I have been trying to locate, create and use positive modes which reject the repressive elements of dominant culture. I am looking for forms and processes which project and reassert those aspects of society which—though of essential value—have been devalued and restricted to women and the home.

As I become more sensitive to those aspects of design which reinforce repressive attitudes and behavior, I increasingly question the desirability of simplicity and clarity. The thrust to control almost inevitably operates through simplification. Control is undermined by ambiguity, choice and complexity because subjective factors in the user become more effective and the user is invited to participate. Participation undermines control. The oversimplified, the unremittingly serious, the emphatically "rational" are the consistent attitudes associated with work adopted by our major institutions and the men and few women who inhabit them. In the circle of cause and effect, these attitudes are reinforced and reproduced as they are visually and physically extended into our environment.

One means of simplification is to assign attributes to various groups and thereby reinforce divisions. The restriction of certain behavior to the home and the designation of women as the sole custodians of a range of human characteristics create a destructive imbalance. The design arts reinforce this imbalance by projecting the "male" tone only in the public world of our large institutions: business, science, the military and even education, valuing their anonymous, authoritarian aspects and separating themselves further and further from the private world, thus continuing to isolate women, female experience and "female" values.

Designers are most often taught to reduce ideas to their essence, but in fact that process too often results in the reduction of the ideas to only one of their parts. "Designed" has almost come to mean exclusive, universal, clear and simple, rather than inclusive, personal, ambiguous and complex. As a result visual design generally means imagery with a single, large image, one major headline, and any explanatory information in a block of small type. A more organizational style and more visual material would insure enough complexity to entice readers, who normally dart away with someone else's encapsulated vision, to remain long enough and openly enough with the information to create ideas of their own.

Mass media communications: a diagram of simplified separations.

The mass media have a tradition of visual simplification in order to isolate their messages to attract attention. Such simplification denies the complexity of life's experience, for while simple statements, familiar and repeated imagery sell the product and the idea most efficiently, they also reinforce restricting separations.

In advertising, women are described as, or permitted to be, laughing, crying, doubting, making mistakes, hesitating: women alone are seen as nurturing or as providing emotional support for children and men. When, for example, a company presents itself in a service capacity or as particularly accommodating, it uses a female figure and reinforces traditional attitudes by this symbolic imagery. The iconography for men is equally rigid. Men in work situations are shown as serious, decisive, professional, assured. No emotions, no fantasy; the few moments of relaxation or emotion permitted to men are relegated to leisure and the home. Likewise, the home becomes devalued as a place where no serious work can be done. As the woman is virtually seen only in the home, she too is devalued. By depicting woman as exclusively emotional, doubting, cooperating and helping others, by only showing these activities in private, in the home, the polarities not only of what men and women are thought to be, but where it is appropriate to be that way, are reinforced and legitimized. In fact, the very characteristics which are allowed women in the home prevent "success" in the competitive public sector.

If the idea and the design are simple, complete and set, there is no opportunity to bring one's own values to the forms, let alone challenge one's attitudes and assumptions about men, women, work, and home. If there is no ambiguity the eye is attracted once, the message understood and accepted quickly. When visual material is ambiguous the different nuances often encourage multiple and alternative reactions to the same communication, and the viewer is encouraged to make an effort to extrapolate, to participate. But the client seldom includes this as part of the problem and designers themselves most often limit the problems to be solved in an effort to arrive at a potent image. For most clients and designers, the problem does not include the encouragement of a thinking audience.

The Modern movement encouraged simplicity and clarity of form, a mode which was embraced by some of the most creative and intelligent designers. It became fashionable to simplify for the clarity and power of the image, but as design becomes fashion, simplification becomes pernicious. This simplification in form and process leads too often to restriction and limiting separations and boundaries. By allowing for more complexity and participation, designers could avoid visual authoritarianism.

Publications: some alternative modes.

The movements of the sixties questioned the structure and institutions that engender

unquestioning conformity. The youth, hippie, counter-culture movements helped validate some repressed "female" values, and encouraged the growth of the women's movement.

Alternative modes which pointed out the limitations of one-directional channels of communication began to be developed and modern offset printing began to be used as a model for participatory politics. *The Whole Earth Catalog,* by compiling reviews of goods and services recommended by a large number of contributors across the country, helped reestablish the value of individual subjectivity. In a special issue of the *Aspen Times* devoted to the International Design Conference in Aspen, I distributed cards on which the participants themselves could express their diverse attitudes toward the conference. An increasing number of periodicals have guest editors, guest designers—*Radical Software, Design Quarterly, Arts in Society* and others. As in the structure of the *Whole Earth Catalog* and the IDCA issue of the *Aspen Times,* special issues of ongoing publications provide alternatives to the creative input of the established designers and editors and expand the number of sources of information.

Volume 7 number 3 of *Arts in Society,* devoted to the formation of the California Institute of the Arts, was composd of several types of visual and textual material organized in waves of information. As the California Institute of the Arts was yet to open

and not completely defined, I created a tentative, fragmented organization in an effort to encourage the reader to participate in the ultimate conceptualization of this new community of the arts. My intention was to supply a multiplicity of information which would create a struggle for the readers making their perception more meaningful. As we become more used to ambiguity and complexity in design and content and are encouraged to participate, the more we will be able to support the formation and expression of individual, subjective conclusions to advocate the sharing of authority.

If the design material is organized in fragments, multiple peaks rather than a single climatic moment, it has a quality and rhythm which may parallel women's ontological experience, particularly her experience of time. Although I used this fragmented organization in an effort to reflect a community of the arts in formation and to encourage the reader to participate, I realized simultaneously that this form of visual organization corresponds to what is considered by our society to be women's way of working.

There are several genres of women's work, quilts and blankets for example, which are an assemblage of fragments pieced together whenever there is time, which are in both their method of creation as well as in their aesthetic form, visually organized into many centers. The quilting bee, as well as the quilt itself, is an example of an

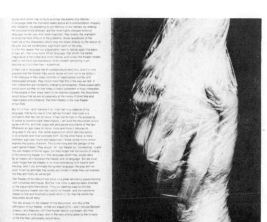
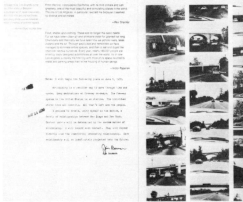

Eight pages from *Arts in Society,* V7#3.

"Horse" Crazy Quilt, made in 1887 by Helen Mary Rounsville in Fowlerville, Michigan. "She raised horses and loved her garden." From the collection of Mary Strickler's Quilt, a shop at 936 "B" Street, San Rafael, Cal.

essentially non-hierarchical organization. Certainly the quality of time in a woman's life, particularly if she is not involved in the career thrust toward fame and fortune, is distinct from the quality of time experienced by men and women who are caught up in the "progress" of a career.

The linearity of time is foreign to the actual structure of a day as well as to the rhythm of women's monthly biological time. Thought processes released from the distortions of mechanical progress are complex, repetitive and permeated with the multiple needs of others as well as oneself. Unbounded relationships cause most women to think not only about work, but about the groceries needed for dinner, a child's dental problems, etc., in between thoughts about work. Women's tasks in the home are equally varied and open-ended—child-rearing is the classic example—while a man's work in the home has a beginning and an end, it has specific projects, like the fixing of windows, appliances or plumbing. The assemblage of fragments, the organization of forms in a complex matrix, suggests depth and intensity as an alternative to progress.

When the design arts are called upon to project aspects of the women's movement it is a particularly appropriate time to challenge existent assumptions about form and process. When I was asked by a group of women artists to design a special issue of *Everywoman,* a feminist newspaper, I tried to incorporate the visual projection of the egalitarian, collective form of small group process. In weekly meetings women throughout the country meet in small groups, and talk in turn so that those easily dissuaded from speaking by more vibrant, dominant personalities, are assured of being heard. In this *Everywoman* design I avoided the associations of space and length of article with quality, and gave each woman a large photo of herself and a two-page spread. I tried to link the spreads visually and to make no spread dominant. Looking alike, the articles did not visually compete with each other for the reader's attention: it was left to the reader to discern differences which might be subjectively more meaningful.

Designing a structure that will encourage participating, non-hierarchical, non-authoritarian relationships between the designer, client and user, also results in visual and physical forms that are outside the mainstream of design as much as these ideas and attitudes are outside mainstream culture. Publications designed in such a way look different from the way our national publications look; this difference is much less the result of creating another style than of designing structures which encourage other values. As desirable as it is that these values become infused into society, such design structures are often modest in appearance rather than bold. Perhaps the importance of dynamic visual stimuli should be questioned, and quiet literary forms be reevaluated.

In trying to create visual forms and processes which reflect the political form of the women's movement, its collectivity and consciousness, a designer must adopt a structure which encourages a broad base of participation. One of the ways women artists can express their experiences, feelings, and needs directly to a larger audience than the loft-gallery-museum-going elite is to use mass media technology so that more people could see and respond to their images. Because of the separation of art and design in our schools and in most critical publications, artists are often unfamiliar with and sometimes scorn offset lithography as an appropriate form in which to do their work.

In response to the restricting separation of our disciplines, I have joined with two other women, an artist and an art historian, in an effort to create an alternative learning situation for women in the arts—*The Feminist Studio Workshop.* In designing the mailer announcing this experimental project I created a matrix of the quotations and imagery which were influencing our ideas about the formation of *The Feminist Studio Workshop.* As the mailer is opened, information written by each of us and a photograph is presented. As the reader unfolds the mailer, new bands of written and visual work, by women past and present, are revealed followed by a progression containing some of our own work, work done with students, and text written collectively about the goals of the workshop. The viewer can read any or all of the quotes, can connect the images in any way personally meaningful, and we hope that she will be enticed to respond.

We each chose the material which we wanted to represent us; the quote which best describes my feelings about being a woman designer is from Virginia Woolf's *Three Guineas,*

> *Behind us lies the patriarchal system; the private house, with its nullity, its immorality, its hypocrisy, its servility. Before us lies the public world, the professional system, with its possessiveness, its jealousy, its pugnacity, its greed . . . The question we put to you is how can we enter the professions and yet remain civilized human beings . . .*

I have begun to try to find an answer for myself as a woman designer. Designers must work in two ways. We must create visual and physical designs which project social forms but simultaneously we must create the social forms which will demand new visual and physical manifestations. The work in the design arts which I have described are products of situations in which the designer was to give physical form to efforts devoted to creating new social contexts. In these cases the major thrust was to rethink assumptions; profit was not a major consideration, the budget was modest, and the audience (unfortunately) was often limited. The designer was exempt from the pressures that make it difficult for larger money-making projects, to see the connection between effectiveness in shaping our consciousness, the forms and processes which might encourage values and financial viability.

In its need to grow and present its point of view, *Ms.* magazine appears to have looked to the successful mainstream publications for models rather than to those special interest publications of the sixties. The need for color advertising for survival as a mass magazine, makes demands on the size and paper used, and it is doubtful that a publication has to be on newsprint and in black and white only in order to express alternative values by its physical form.

But I am less convinced of other assumptions about the forms necessary for survival. I am distressed that the equalized relationships which mark the political form of the women's movement are expressed by *Ms.* only by the equalization of office relationships, rather than challenging the creation of an authoritarian elite by reorganizing other aspects of its structure as well. A combination of the guest editor, guest designer structure used by *Arts in Society, Radical Software, Design Quarterly* and others, and the direct broad-based participation involved in the structure of the *Whole Earth Catalog* and the IDCA *Times* issue might be possible. The formation of a small, closed design and editorial elite and the authority of a centralized geographical location could possibly be broken by creating editorial and design teams in the east, west and midwest. This decentralized structure would also create a vehicle for many different points of view, expressed by the women participating themselves rather than being reported upon by others. This variety and structure would affect the look of the magazine, expressing its theoretical differences. Though attractive and lively as it is, *Ms.'s* form is much more the result of traditional forms and processes than an integral connection with new values of relationship.

My concern with more complex, open, unbounded forms of both the profession of design and its expression relates to ideas about the traditional female role. The inclusiveness, accommodation and service associated with female role—and restricted to women—corresponds with the aspect of design as a helping profession, one in which the designer helps give physical form to the clients' needs. Being a designer and a woman becomes most compatible for me when the client's needs are much like my own. This was true when I designed the *Arts in Society* issue about the formation of the California Institute of the Arts. In this instance I was the designer for an issue about the institution where I would be teaching.

In the resurgence of feminism in the sixties, it appeared important that we proclaim that we can be aggressive as well as passive, capable of primary responsibility as well as being dependent, competitive as well as accommodating. But somehow in the demands for equality and even superiority some have lost sight of this concept, creating instead an either/or conceptualization. Reexamining some aspects of the design arts and being more aware of being a woman, it seems that the complexity and contradiction, the "female" values, could be revalidated and reinforced. It appears to me that it is the "male" tone prescribed for the public world of our major institutions that makes the profession of designer an ambiguous enterprise for a woman. The present professional system does not encourage the emergence of the values restricted to women and the home into the public world and fosters instead—among designers, at least—a kind of style-conscious creation of "pretty" objects detached from alternative social contexts. The professional system in which the choice is between being a commercial star or a commercial hack does not encourage design for social change.

Futures: some alternative modes.

One way for the design arts to alter the public world is to develop images of the future which embody alternative values. To do this we must know what forms most communicate "female" values and which devalue the female experience and cannot incorporate such modes as emotionality, complexity and supportive cooperation. The difficulty of infusing positive aspects of woman's experience in the private home into the public work world is exemplified by our inability to imagine a perfect or radically different society. The inevitability of reproducing ourselves rather than a new society could be avoided as we think of the values we wish to project into the new world.

The tradition of utopia in the Renaissance appears "female" in tone—supportive, cooperative and gentle. Sir Thomas More was unable openly to criticize his contemporary society and consequently used satire in juxtaposition to his vision, thus softening what would have been a more obvious and harsher evaluation. This element of satire allowed the people of his time to aspire toward the values which More was articulating by comparing their own society with his invention of Utopia.

While early utopian visions were pastoral, later ones were more mechanical, developing as they did in conjunction with man's ability to control nature. By the twentieth century, control first of nature, then of man himself, is not only a possibility but to a large extent an actuality, and utopias became transformed from aspirations to predictions and warnings. Fourier was perhaps the only nineteenth century utopian thinker who tried to envision social and physical structures which encouraged a variety of human response rather than building social forms which either eliminated certain behavior patterns or controlled them.

Most modern visions of the future reflect and project the rigid separations of male and female, work and leisure, public and private, that the design profession has so often reinforced in its mass communications. To warn society of what could become the inevitable outgrowths of contemporary patterns, Wells, Orwell, and Huxley described negative visions of the future. The total restriction and control of people's behavior in these anti-utopias represents a critique of existing society. The unique characters who oppose the social and political order are rendered absolutely impotent and are eventually edited out of these fictional societies.

Systems that achieve reliability—as virtually all dystopian systems do—through conditioning cause people to be simplified and controlled. What dismays me most is that the kinds of behavior most frequently eliminated in these visions are the "imperfect" characteristics which have been defined as "female," partially because they are not simple, limited or predictable. They imply choice, inclusiveness and complexity, which, as I have pointed out before, undermine control. These dystopian visions warn of futures in which men and women are indistinguishable—they are all made in that narrowest definition of "male". We find a future projected from modes of behavior designated for the public realm of work while the characteristics of home and women are deleted.

It is the absence of other "female" futures that renders the utopian vision negative. Without a concerted effort to imagine alternative futures, we will have a future in which individual choice is eliminated along with emotions, ambiguity and fantasy. For if we continue to eliminate female values in an effort to warn society of impending futures and make such visions real by their artful vividness, then, in this editing, it is humanism which is finally, totally eradicated.

I would not reiterate such dire visions of the future if I did not feel that there are some realistic alternatives and that these alternatives are somehow involved with the rediscovery and projection of female experience. There seems to be an intrinsic relationship between the communitarian aspects of the women's movements and fanciful human utopian visions. Why are there so few positive visions of the future reflecting female experience despite the fact that there have been communitarian efforts (Mother Ann of the Shakers, for example) in which women have played a major role? It appears that it is even more difficult for women to fantasize about a future when their effectiveness on

the present is limited to daily life in the home. And perhaps, women's more visible contribution to unique, prototypical utopian communities is a reflection of this experience of time in the home.

It seems to me that the integration of design and feminism has implications for the future and it is the opportunity and responsibility of women to use this area to infuse "female" values into our culture. As there are virtually no blueprints for the future by woman based on female experience, we must project a future responsive to our needs if we are to have a future at all.

In a women's studies class I initiated at the California Institute of the Arts, the women have begun to read utopian literature, to look at the theory and design of communitarian environments and to create images of the future from their own individual, personal perspective. Not surprisingly, the first

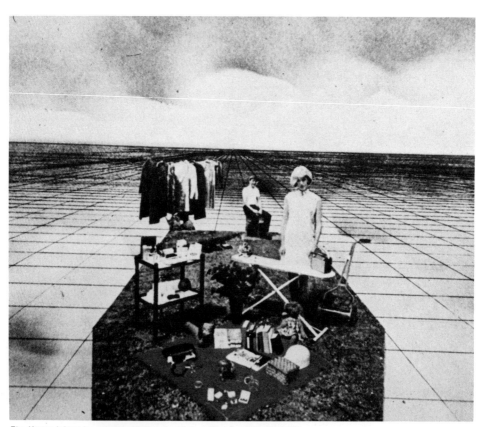

The Happy Island by a group of women artists called Superstudio, 1972.

images that are being made exhibit fears identical to those of the dystopian writers. We look forward to the creation of images which will disseminate female values presently minimized and even threatened with eradication.

Projects like this blur the role distinctions between designer and user, expert and amateur. They increase the number of participants in the life of society and provide a successful model for non-hierarchical organization. You the audience can now look at the few images which have been created, evaluate them and make choices creating your own personal alternative views of the future. You can reject the contemporary status quo and reach out for new forms through which to shape wished-for worlds. Together we can salvage values which have been eliminated from contemporary life as well as project new values and ideas which come from our own bodies

and experiences. Women have learned that it is impossible to live without real communication either with others or with themselves. To some extent the very process by which we take responsibility, not only for our own choices, our own lives, but for society as well, is a new form which brings a humane future closer. □

*This article was written and edited from lecture notes first given at Hunter College in the fall of 1972. The formulation of my ideas about design and its relationship to feminism is in part a response to information from the following sources:

C. Wright Mills, *Power, Politics and People* (New York: Ballantine Books, 1962). Originally the article "Man in the Middle: The Designer" was published in the review *Industrial Design* (November, 1958).

Amos Rapaport and Robert E. Kantor, "Complexity and Ambiguity in Environmental Design," *American Institute of Planners Journal* (July, 1967).

Juliet Mitchell, *Women's Estate*, Pantheon Books, (New York, 1971).

Robert Boguslaw, *The New Utopians: A Study of System Design and Social Change* (Englewood Cliffs, N.J.; Prentice-Hall, 1965).

Air Force Academy, Houston, Texas. Architects: Skidmore, Owings & Merrill.

SOCIAL ORGANIZATION AND DESIGN

Studio for artist David Jacobs. Architect: Noel Phyllis Birkby.

Dolores Hayden is an assistant professor in the Department of Architecture at M.I.T. and is currently working on a book entitled The Living Building *which is about the planning and design of nineteenth century communes. She is a founder of Women in Architecture, Landscape Architecture and Planning and works with the M.I.T. Community Projects Laboratory.*

Sheila de Bretteville is a designer and instructor in design at the California Institute of the Arts. She currently is doing a project on utopian alternatives.

Clare Spark-Loeb is Associate Director of Drama and Literature at Pacifica KPFK-FM in North Hollywood, California.

Clare Spark-Loeb: I wanted to make an observation to begin with. Many people in their critiques of feminism have accused it of being a basically middle-class movement, and one aspect of serious feminist thought that interests me is the creation of alternatives to present relationships, social organization, design—and that's going to be the topic of our discussion. Dolores, what is WALAP?

Dolores Hayden: WALAP is Women in Architecture, Landscape Architecture and Planning. It's a group started in the Boston-Cambridge area in the fall of 1971. At that time I had just left the Harvard Graduate School of Design with my degree in architecture. I was looking for a job and finding that as a woman I was really unemployable in a very tight job market. WALAP was an attempt to find other women professionals in environmental design. I hoped we would begin to talk about our common problems and define legal strategies and political strategies for reevaluating our situation as women. A few of us began to explore the sorts of jobs we were eligible for, whether or not we wanted those jobs, whether the professions were really serving the needs of socially conscious people generally, as well as the needs of women. And in time the organization grew to include over a hundred people in the area and we began to overcome the isolation that each one of us had felt as a woman alone in those fields.

Sheila de Bretteville: Is there a relationship between your having started WALAP and your work in trying to understand physical form and how it can contain social attitudes and social values?

Dolores Hayden: I think there is although it wasn't a terribly conscious relationship to begin with. When I finished my graduate education, I really thought that it was necessary to take a very traditional architectural job and make my way in the field as men expected to make their way in the field. And finding that there was serious discrimination in employment forced me to evaluate whether that was what I wanted to do. I had been involved in various women's projects for two to three years before founding WALAP—trying to change sexist academic hiring-firing policies at Harvard and participating in a consciousness-raising group which included women from other fields. I began to think that if I got together with other women it might be possible to see whether there was a general demand for alternatives or whether it was just my need for alternatives. After having been involved in WALAP, I found that the kinds of alternatives that people wanted were really very diverse. Perhaps the best thing about WALAP was not bringing women into established firms, which it did to some extent, but rather allowing a lot of other women the freedom to think about what they might do outside of this. And I think that WALAP gave me a sense of support for my own work so that I could begin to do research and writing in areas that I felt were meaningful.

Sheila de Bretteville: Most utopian literature tends to either provide an alternative which creates an aspirational level or an alternative which is a warning about what kind of future may be in store for us.

The question I really wanted to ask is this— are alternatives being acted out in communitarian environments? Can you find in the relationship of women to those environments something which would allow you to make projections about possible future alternatives?

Dolores Hayden: Communitarian environments interested me as the experiments of people who were willing to put their lives on the line and create communities which would be examples of practical socialism— actually do this, not simply write about it or draw it up. People who took themselves off to the country and spent ten or twenty years working it out. I found myself very sympathetic to this kind of total life commitment as opposed to intellectual commitment to an idea of social change while one actually lives in a very confined way. The main difference between utopian and communitarian thinking is that utopian thinkers are always spinning out fantasies in a kind of idealized space, whereas the communitarians work with life space and deal with the question of how spaces make people feel about their lives. If there is one thing that I find particularly bothersome about contemporary architecture in the United States, it is the sense that there is a terrific striving for an ideal building, a kind of monumental closed statement which is made by a single designer. I am much more interested in a sort of gradual approach to developing environments and environmental form, interested in historical preservation and rehabili-

tation, in the growth and change of physical form. And I'm interested in the ways that groups with very specific political ideas can use physical form as an organizing tool. In order to really understand this better, I began to do communitarian research, hoping to find what had happened when large groups of people tried to design environments collectively over a long period of time.

Clare Spark-Loeb: Dolores, can I ask you a question about your research? Were the historians interested in the issues that you needed to explore, particularly with your own philosophy of design?

Dolores Hayden: Well, some historians have taken to deriding the whole movement as a kind of eccentric happening and looking at people who became involved in communitarian experiments as fanatics and fools who couldn't fit in anywhere else. But, in the nineteenth century creating a communitarian socialist settlement was considered a very respectable strategy for social change; it fell midway between gradualist reform of existing institutions and violent revolution. And it was based on an analogy between the community and mechanical inventions. If the model community was a successful invention, it could be duplicated and mass produced. If this happened in the United States where the frontier was moving westward, then the entire country could be influenced by one superior community which people copied. Although this may seem rather naive in retrospect, I think in the 1830's and 1840's in the United States it made a certain amount of sense.

In contrast to some historians who take a very sarcastic approach, many people who have been involved in writing social history or religious history have often done a very sympathetic job. But they have concerned themselves more with ideas than with environment and they have usually failed to deal with the question of the physical invention of the model community. They have dealt very well with the social invention, with all the ins and outs of creating commitment and creating new kinds of family structures, new sorts of economic rewards. The working out of socialism in practice is all very well documented. But the idea that there would have to be a special sort of landscape design and a special sort of building design to make people feel that they were in an alternative society has never been examined very carefully. The architectural historians who have looked at the material are few and far between, but they've generally taken the approach that the only communitarian buildings worth studying were the very few monumental buildings in a given community. Discussions of whether or not there was Greek revival influence in a given building completely miss the point, of course. They ignore the question of how you organize space for social

Top: Shaker Communal Dwelling (1830), Church Family, Hancock, Mass.
Bottom: North American Phalanx Communal Dwelling (1849-52), Phalanx, N.J. Photos by William Logan.

change in favor of analyzing some particular building's style. Although style in some ways could become part of a strategy for social change, it usually was not the most important community issue.

Sheila de Bretteville: Would the people who have access to the research that you are doing and to your attitude of forms having meanings—not only meanings but actually encouraging change—change within their own lives the forms or would they have to create entire communities in order to do that?

Dolores Hayden: I think that there are many immediate applications of the research that I'm doing. The kinds of things that I was involved in as a designer which made me want to do this research were as varied as housing for migrant workers, a large apartment complex in New York City, and a small commune for divinity students in Boston. The common element in all those projects was needing spaces for people to come together, spaces which would make it easy rather than difficult for people to express in their life style their commitment to social change. Having done the communitarian research, I think that there are results which can be useful to community groups working on any sort of environmental design. There are patterns of organization—visual diagrams of the arrangement of spaces, the relationship of certain kinds of spaces to circulation, to outdoors, to community, privacy, dining, living, working, sleeping, whatever, and those particular patterns can be applied to other design situations very easily by simply finding a program where the requirements are similar and then using whatever details seem to be appropriate.

Sheila de Bretteville: Do you feel that these forms will have to come from changed patterns of living and changed attitudes and behaviors or would the forms encourage people to change attitudes and behaviors and the way they are living?

Dolores Hayden: Well, I don't believe that the forms produce the change. I think that if you have people who want a specific change, then the form will often help to make that easier and to make it possible.

Sheila de Bretteville: So you're not inflating the role of design?

Dolores Hayden: No, I think the utopian approach is to say that you create a new form and that makes everything all right. In Thomas More's *Utopia* you have a city of identical houses and therefore everyone is equal. I think you have to create the social and economic situation where people wish to be more equal and then think about the kind of physical environment they need to make a statement about wanting that equality, to make it possible for them to live comfortably with greater equality—given also that families are different, that individuals are different, that you probably don't want everyone in this society in an identical house because it would really be totalitarian.

Sheila de Bretteville: The only thing that's unfortunate in what you have said is that you come back to having to make the attitudes change first before you can change anything else.

Dolores Hayden: Well, I don't think that it's an absolutely either/or question. Social change is a process and a long, difficult, on-going process. Environments can hinder or aid that process. There is an interdependent relationship which is what social change and environmental design are both really all about. My book, *The Living Building*, will provide specific patterns for people who know they want a different design but don't know quite what the possibilities are. But even more important are the case histories of six different communities that struggled to create their own communitarian environments. These case histories document the design process and show the connections between social change and developing physical design over ten years, fifty years, a hundred years. These are chiefly success stories and they are meant to inspire people who are involved in changing the environment, whether it's creating something as small as a commune for six people or whether it's something as large as a community center for two hundred people.

Clare Spark-Loeb: What were the six communities you researched?

Dolores Hayden: Well, I have been looking at the Shakers and their community at Hancock, Massachusetts; the North American Phalanx, which was a Fourierite community in Monmouth County, New Jersey; the Oneida Perfectionists in upstate New York;

the Mormons in Nauvoo, Illinois; Union Colony Number One in Greeley, Colorado; and a Marxist community at Llano del Rio, California.

Clare Spark-Loeb: What were your sources for your documentation since as you said earlier the approach which the regular historians had taken did not give you the information which you were seeking specifically?

Dolores Hayden: It was necessary to go back to the sites and look at the remains which in some cases were really substantial; to begin to read the community minutes; to read the letters and diaries of community members to find out how they felt about the environment; to look at the communities' budgets; to examine old maps and old site plans; to see how the communities had bought land, how they developed the land, how they made decisions on where to site the factories, fields and dwellings. Each community generally considered itself a sovereign state in miniature which would necessarily incorporate very diverse kinds of land use for a small settlement. Communitarians also generally considered that it was necessary to cultivate the land as perfectly as possible so that a visitor crossing the boundaries from the outside world into the community would see automatically that there had been a change, that the model settlement was a more perfect place. So landscape design was very important. In terms of how the buildings were created—sometimes there were existing building plans, sometimes there were old photographs, in some cases I have been able to interview people who were either involved in the construction of the dwellings or could remember them from their childhood. There are a few Shakers in Maine and New Hampshire, particularly a woman named Sister Mildred Barker, who helped me understand that the Shaker attitude towards existing buildings was that they must continue to be perfected even though the community seemed as perfect to me as anyone could possibly want it to be. And I interviewed a woman in New Jersey who remembered the buildings from the North American Phalanx from her childhood around the turn of the century. She was able to describe to me the interior of a dining room wing which had been torn down around 1910. As she described it, I made sketches and she cor-

rected the sketches until finally we came to what she thought was an accurate description of that building which is now missing. The process of getting information has been very exciting.

Clare Spark-Loeb: Is there anything in common between these various communities concerning families and marriage or was there a variety of arrangements?

Dolores Hayden: It's tremendously varied. The main lesson that I have learned from studying communitarians is that there is absolutely no clear answer or prescription for successful social change. The kinds of social arrangements that people wished and the kinds of physical arrangements which they designed were very diverse. The Shakers were celibate, the Oneidans practiced what they called complex marriage, which meant that anyone in the community was able to invite anyone else in the community to have sex with them. The dwelling of the Shakers has the women living on one side of the building and the men on the other. Communal rooms cross the axis of the building, but there is always an invisible line which separates men from women. In the mansion of the Oneida Community they have a completely different arrangement for complex marriage. There are between fourteen and twenty-eight single rooms grouped around a sitting room. The sitting room provides a sort of neighborhood feeling for those fourteen to twenty-eight people. It also provides a kind of policing situation for complex marriage in that members were expected to "keep in circulation;" they were not expected to have an exclusive relationship with any one individual. They saw sex as something which enabled people to spread love through the entire community. Then there were some communities where members were interested in keeping the nuclear family intact. I think they generally had quite a bit of trouble because the instinct for private property and family territory was very much tied to the traditional sense of the nuclear family. For the Mormons and for the Union Colony in Greeley, Colorado, the nuclear family was sort of a constant force of pulling people back into a private situation rather than encouraging them to join the communal situation. The Mormons got around that in some ways by establishing polygamy.

Clare Spark-Loeb: One-sided polygamy.

Dolores Hayden: Yes, there was still the very real problem of male-domination in the community and question of whether women were actually shared property rather than full members in their own right. Most communitarians were interested in the question of the status of women and the status of children. Many argued for a reform of society along feminist lines. The head of the Shakers was Ann Lee who was considered the female counterpart of Christ. The Shakers felt that only after there had been a male messiah and a female messiah could the millenium begin. They were organized with a dual hierarchy with two men and two women occupying every position of leadership. Some of the writings of Shaker eldresses are wonderful feminist tracts describing how life for a young woman in rural New England in the early nineteenth century was terribly confining—she could only marry and rock the cradle. But if she chose to join the Shakers, they claimed that she would be treated as a person in her own right with full possibilities for expression of her talents and intelligence. The Oneidans were pretty concerned about women's liberation as well, and probably the North American Phalanx too. In both of those communities the women wore trouser suits and had short hair and played some role as directors and administrators of the community. Although they were never fully equal with the men, they were certainly making attempts.

Sheila de Bretteville: I'm curious about the demise of some of these communities, particularly the North American Phalanx. Which ones were ended by forces which are present today?

Dolores Hayden: The small isolated community is always in difficulty because in order to define itself as separate and special, it has to be set apart from the larger society. Then the question of how people will be proselytized is a problem. Will they come to the community, think it's a success, and want to join? If they want to join, how many new members will overwhelm the original community and totally dilute its impact? If they aren't allowed to join, if it's suggested that they go off and start another community of their own, will they be able to keep up the original group's creative force? Perhaps I should talk about one "success" and one "failure."

In the North American Phalanx there was a constant struggle between patrons and members. Many of the leading intellectuals and writers of the 1840's were interested in Fourierism—people like Nathaniel Hawthorne and Ralph Waldo Emerson, who took an interest in Brook Farm, Horace Greeley, publisher of the New York *Tribune,* and Marcus Spring, who was a well-known abolitionist and a wealthy New York merchant. These were the sort of people who found radicalism chic and who had a very specific and very architectural idea of what the model community should be like. They saw the future North American Phalanx as a huge dwelling with a facade about a half-mile long. They talked about community in terms of building a factory into which they would put the people and create harmony by the fact that the physical organization of the building was set up to make the community work.

Eventually the patrons offered money to the members if they would build a monumental dwelling. They withdrew their offer when the people of the North American Phalanx said that they would rather buy some new farm equipment and build their buildings gradually, piece by piece, according to their needs and collective ability. Eventually that community failed financially because of the split between the outside supporters and the actual committed members.

Then Marcus Spring, one of the patrons, decided that he would create another community more to his liking, the Raritan Bay Union. He hired an architect and spent forty to fifty thousand dollars building a huge overwrought brick phalanstery which would probably have accommodated eighty people. Opposite this communal dwelling, he built himself a private house. I have a sketch showing Marcus Spring's house facing the community mansion across an expanse of flowers. And I think it suggests the problem of really coming to terms with wealth, individualism, and elitism. It doesn't matter how many meetings you go to or how much rhetoric you lay out about the ideal community—if you still want to live in your own mansion and have it across the way, then social change is really never going to occur.

In terms of both communitarian success and private property, I would also like to talk about the Mormons as communitarians. Most literature about communitarian experiments does not discuss the Mormons and I think this is because the Mormons actually succeeded in carrying the communitarian theory to its logical extreme. They were influenced by the Shakers, by the followers of a woman named Jemimah Wilkinson who founded a community called Jerusalem, and by the Rappists, German communists from Pennsylvania. They founded three or four socialist communities where they were really struggling to balance private property against communal ownership and to find some form of socialism which did not discourage the rich converts from bringing in all their money. They finally came up with a system of tithing to support the church and church activities, and a system of cooperative agriculture. Yet private property was allowed and private business was encouraged. In several places the Mormons didn't succeed. They were persecuted and driven from Illinois, but in Salt Lake City they found the complete spatial vacuum, a location on the American frontier which appeared too unattractive to appeal to competing settlers. Within thirty years they had founded four hundred new communities, each one based on the Plat of the City of Zion, which was Joseph Smith's original drawing of the ideal Mormon community. And they developed a successful social system—people in successful communities were called to lead the establishment of new communities. But, ironically, this very success resulted in the Mormon's being omitted from most of the literature on communitarian settlements. They didn't fit the model of an idealistic failure in the way that they came to terms with the capitalist society around them.

Sheila de Bretteville: In proclaiming itself as perfect the communitarians might project a negative force rather than a positive force. I think people respond negatively to something saying it's perfect because it points you out as imperfect.

Dolores Hayden: I think what one wants to say is that it's an approach to being better.

There are five things that I found to be typical of communitarians, although maybe this is just an attempt to organize a very complicated subject. But one characteristic is perfectability, a sense that human nature and the built environment and all aspects of life could be better than they are now. And the second is accountability—which is closely related to perfectability—the sense that each person must struggle in the present to make alternatives possible. The third is collectivity, the sense that you don't struggle alone but that you join with other people who are supporting each other.

Fourth is uniqueness—which again is somewhat related to perfectability—the sense that a given community would have to express its difference from the rest of society by creating a distinctive, recognizable style of life. And then the last is credibility, the sense that whatever was done in the model community had to be done so consistently that it could be duplicated elsewhere. Credibility connected the communitarians' experiments with the ideal of social change. And I think in some sense these characteristics are all present as qualities or aspirations in contemporary communes.

Sheila de Bretteville: How can you as a practicing architect help those who are beginning to work out solutions?

Dolores Hayden: What's excited me very much is that the research is not only useful to me in clarifying my own ideas about design and people's collective participation in design. Having satisfied myself that it's possible for a group of people to create an alternate life-space which really helps them politically and socially, I now have a great deal of information about how that can be done. I have begun to work with a few community groups—consulting, making the information available, trying to help them to be more self-conscious about their design process—to see design as a political process and to see it also as a process which will have a physical result that they will feel good about. And, in this context, I have begun to feel good about the possibilities of being a "social" architect.

Sheila de Bretteville: I know that in the last decade it has not been unusual for young

Field House, Camp Kenwood, Potter Place, N.H. Architects: Goody & Clancy; Joan Goody, Partner-in-charge.
This simple structure covers a large (70' x 110') area with an extremely economical structural system.
It houses rainy day and evening athletics for a large camp.

architects to elect to work with community groups. I have often felt that they have come to that decision from a stylistic point of view as opposed to one of social process and their radicalism is not unlike the kind of radicalism that you described when describing Spring and Greeley. Could you be specific in illuminating the difference between your approach to community work and the design process, and those who do community work from a particularly stylistic inclination of chic, radical point of view?

Dolores Hayden: When I first worked with community groups, I found there was a tremendous conflict between trying to find out what their needs were and trying to do something as a designer. I was trying to use my design experience, which presumably gave me a better sense of taste or style; wishing to impose my requirements on the community; wondering how fast I could educate them to understand that a certain form was really the perfect expression of their policy or program. Naturally it was really frustrating because often the community groups which had the most exciting programs had the least money and were always requiring people to scavenge materials. The possibilities of creating unique forms were always going rapidly downhill. I think that it's not only really possible to work as a designer in the sense of creating special forms and to work with a community group as well. One can only work successfully with a community group by becoming part of it. The art is probably in the process and not in the product; that the better the process is, the more involved people become with creating spaces where it feels good to be. As the architect becomes invisible, as there is no possibility for a signature or for a four-page spread in any one of the professional journals, the process is probably more successful, the community is more in control and therefore the physical form is more likely to be a true reflection of the community's own political process. This goes very much against the ideas of most designers.

Sheila de Bretteville: Certainly, it's a very radical point of view in that most people who are creative tend to think that their creation comes out of some source which must be preserved as a separate individual and must be acclaimed from that point of view

and that it cannot be molded from within a community situation.

Dolores Hayden: I think something very exciting happens when art begins to merge with life or the political process. The kind of creative satisfaction that comes from organizing spaces or from organizing a facade is a real expressive pleasure. One can hoard that expressive pleasure as an individual, or one can begin to share that expressive pleasure with a group of people. And the potential of shared collective expression in terms of creating joy, happiness, all the good things of art, is really much greater than the potential of making one architect happy sitting at a drawing board somewhere.

Sheila de Bretteville: I think that besides the tradition of individuality and that tradition being tied to the artist is the fear of quality being lost if one shares the design or art process, the fear of loss of control.

Dolores Hayden: I think there is one lesson that I have learned from the communitarian research which has really reassured me on this point. Many of the communities, in order to survive economically, decided that they must create a number of technical inventions which they could produce, so they had very large community meetings in which people were encouraged to design new products which the community could manufacture. And by this process of generating ideas in a supportive situation, and then having people improve each other's ideas and refine them, communities came up with far more creative and original solutions for industrial design than any comparable groups of two hundred or three hundred people anywhere else in the population.

Sheila de Bretteville: I think it's using competition in a positive sense, rather than individuals competing with each other to make more and more unique things. When they work together the competition works to make the thing itself become better and better. I think many of the forces that are active on an individualistic point of view within our own culture are forces which are viable and should not be turned off but which can be redirected and actually have greater fruits if they were to be done on a collective base. ☐

POETRY

Martha Graham—"Letter to the World," 1940 (kick). Photo by Barbara Morgan (Scarsdale, NY),
from book, *Barbara Morgan Monograph,* Morgan and Morgan, Inc., 1972.

Constance Urdang

HOW TO DO IT

By fasting
by turning
by looking into the well
by staying out, in good weather, and
watching how the grass grows
in bad weather, fixing
a point on the wall

by holding the breath
by staying awake
by rubbing the body with aromatic oils
by going naked

by troubling the surface of the waters
by opening the eyes unto the stars
by counting stars

by the glass, wherein all images are clear
by the needle, that pricks and lets no one rest
by fire, that burns and is not consumed
by song
by praise
by silence

MOTHER

Outlived herself
In the body of a cat
Old bones rusting through spiky fur

Grown too suspicious
To be taken in by food
Not even cream
Could tempt her

She grew smaller
Crouched in that threadbare pelt
Only her eyes
Were the same
Uncomprehending
Flecks of surprise
In their seaweedy depths

No way out
Of that shabby prison

When he poisoned the cat
The doctor said,
"I hope I go that peaceful."

HER DADDY

is a rough rider!
One gold earring and a Russian leather jacket
above skin-tight pants, her Daddy
rides a hot rod, draws sparks from the superhighways
of her imagining. His belt buckle
switches on the municipal fireworks display.
The little birds who did not fly south
live in his black beard.
From his breast he tears nesting materials
for small nocturnal burrowing animals.
Crumbs from his lips nourish urchins in vacant lots.
His ring, in the shape of a jewelled fish,
or the single dull black eye of a legendary giant,
protect against evil.
His 7-league boots go marching across her horizons.
And when he laughs, all the teeth in the world
exhibit themselves, white, regular, and predatory.

WHATEVER CAN BE DONE, WILL BE DONE

The boy who is kind to animals
Has tied a firecracker to the cat's tail
He is stoning the spotted bitch he
Is called Wind-Chaser
Yesterday he
Gave bread and broken meat
To the street dogs, his friends

His friends are catching lizards behind the wall
They killed a songbird with their catapults
With the boy who is kind to animals
They set fire to a grasshopper, laughing

Along the road
The children are shaking boxes
Something wants to get out
The mother spits curses
She says we should pay because they are hungry
Wind-Chaser, Eye-of-the-Heart, Comes-Again,
I run away from their baffled eyes

Constance Urdang's forthcoming book,
The Picnic in the Cemetery, *will contain the*
above poems. Her work is frequently seen
in the country's leading magazines.

Maxine Kumin

Maxine Kumin is a novelist as well as a poet and a teacher of creative writing. Her books of poems include The Privilege *and* Halfway.

THIS DAY WILL SELF-DESTRUCT

A man lies down in my mind.
We have just made love.
It went historically well, the kind
of hand-in-glove
expertise team workouts can evoke.
Now we lie still and smoke,
the ashtray on my belly blue
as chicory in the dixie cup
on the deal bureau. True,
it's a borrowed room. Third floor walk-up
as a matter of fact,
foreign enough to enhance the act.
Say it's Grand Forks, where I've never been.
All this takes place in the head,
you understand. I play to win
back wicked afternoons in bed,
old afternoons that were
shadows on the grass longer
than home runs lofted out of the park.
We smoke. The chicory blue goes dark,
the ashtray deepens
and the sun drops
under the rim the way it happens
like a used-up lollipop
and the room goes blind
and a man
a man lies down in my mind.

Blue Room. Photo by Catherine Jansen (Philadelphia). The objects in this room are made with fabric coated in blue print emulsion. The fabric is then contact printed by exposure to the sun using actual objects,

Grace Butcher

POETRY WORKSHOP

The gentle people come
with their shy sharp axes
into my woods,
intent on building meadows.

I shall cover my face
with my own long hair
and breathe my own warm breath
when the cold sun
comes clanging down
through silver holes
in the trembling trees.

Much later . . .
long after dark
I plant redwood seeds
furiously,
while from a distance
two birds come strolling.
It had been such a nice day
they thought they would walk.

Whatever shall I tell them
about their nest
and the way things were
when the trees came down?

ON THE 34th BIRTHDAY OF SPRING

I must read, re-read
the poets (those who know)
and not tie my hair back
so tightly as to feel the ugly strain
at my very roots.

There are leaves to be burned in the spring—
this I can accept,
and glimpses from the corner of my eye
that a fast turn of the head
can never explain.

I must accept the lesser miracle
of crocuses in green grass
after having waited through the winter
for the exploding paradox
of crocuses in snow.

The air will curl like tide
around the deep rock of my body
alone in the bright bed
that faces east.
The shocking space
where you have been, have lain,
will fill, or empty, as the case may be,
and all my struggle with dreams,
my golden fantasies of morning
will not put you there
before you are there.

My children grow;
the spiders creep across my legs.
My hair still fills with sun;
my heart has not loosened or grown small.
My mind is too far in at times;
the geography is black as well as green,
but all the colors grow.

There is the line across my throat
where it has been slashed,
and the muscle deep inside tightens
where the scars heal in great lumps
dissolved by certain touches,
certain tenderness.

I perform the ritual,
dance around myself and sing,
"Alone! Alone!" and worship
at the altars of uncertainty
while spring comes anyhow.

I see the difference the body makes:
the gradual texturing of skin,
the ridges in the fingernails,
and laughter creating problems
around the eyes.
But if I can be as serious
as flowers at work,
and, for moments, as unaware,
that will be the blessing of this spring.
The struggle up from underground
has a shuddering climax
as dirt falls back from the thrust of leaves.

The blossom opens in the frenzied sequence
of time-lapse photography to background music.
I watch myself flowering, flowering.
It is inevitable, I guess,
as long as there is spring
and the dark struggle.

Photo by Judith Eglington, Canada, from her show *Earth Visions*.

INTERVIEW WITH A FRETFUL, AGEING LADY POET

My sadness? . . .
necessary.
It is like fine dark caves
with firefly ceilings
and bottomless still pools
that never empty, never change.

What do you want to know?
My mother drank; my father was busy.
Alone with myself
I found fine, terrible things.
Take them and leave
if you don't understand.
They are all I can offer.

My head scrapes the sky;
poems fall like stars.
My feet know bedrock;
I run and the planet turns.
If you want more than that,
I can't help you.
I have no in between.

My sadness?
You always return to that.
I don't think it bothers anyone.
I've already chosen
my genes and chromosomes;
why not ask why my bones are small!
Leave me alone;
my sadness is neither new nor news.

I have a feeling
no one will outlive me.
No one will see my slow climb finished.
No one even knows the mountain is there.
How can I say, "Please notice my mountain"?
I say instead, "Son, Son," and "Husband."
And they wonder what I mean.

Years from now,
how can I say to the quiet air,
to the stars above the mountain,
"Son . . . Husband . . . ."?
No one will be left to remember.
I will only be ancient;
they will be dead.

I hope there will be more
than a dark wind blowing at the top.
The mountain is not worth this sadness
if there is only a dark wind.

But listen—
do *not* write that down.
Say instead, "She spoke brilliantly
of many things."

Not only a poet and an instructor of English
at Kent State, Grace Butcher is also an
(un-lonely) long distance runner who has won
several prizes on the track. She writes,
"I'm learning to ride a motorcycle now—
a BMW 750, no less."

R. E. Sebenthall

TIGER SLEEPING

It places its two fatal blows
side by side neatly
and rests an appeased head
on them: its body is packed
with deferred power,
suspended tigering:

its eyes close
but its nostrils
watch the wind:

the morsel that passes safely
around it in the grass
has not succeeded by stealth:
on the contrary
has been imagined, considered
and decided against:

the afternoon's hot hand
strokes the tiger's drowse;
but at dusk it will lift its head
and stare off across the plain
where a mile or two away
the appointed impala
has begun to think
of the same waterhole
that is crossing the tiger's mind.

STILL LIFE

Under the embalming varnish,
inside the finishing frame,
there is more going on
than immediately meets the eye.

The edge of a knife continues
to menace, a flower insists
on exuding its odor;
the apple has not given up
nor the lemon completely stalled.

The pheasant that looks so killed
keeps dragging in a sky
that runs like a river;
surfaces are shifting mutinously,
colors pulse and flicker—
nothing's agreed to be still.

*R. E. Sebenthall, who lives in Mt. Horeb,
Wisconsin, is not only a poet but also (under
a pen name) a writer of detective stories.
A book review by her appears elsewhere in
this issue.*

Lisel Mueller

THE FALL OF THE MUSE

Her wings are sold for scrap,
her tiara goes to the museum.
She takes off her purple gown,
her long gloves.
In her underwear she is anyone.

Even when she is naked, they laugh.
it's not enough, they shout,
take off your pubic hair,
mutilate your breasts,
cut off a finger,
put a patch on your left eye.

Now she is one of us.
She laughs the small laugh of the ordinary.
She gives us all equal kisses.
She counts her money at inaugural balls.
She is searched at airports.
She depends on sleeping pills.
She betrays Art with Life.
She lectures on the catharsis of drivel.
She learns about Mount Olympus from quiz shows.

She moves in a circle of victims;
they make her eat her heart in public.
She has been bled so many times
her blood has lost its color.
She comes on the stage on all fours
but insists that her teeth be straightened.

Democratic, she sits with us.
We share the flat bread of affluence,
the suicidal water;
we kill each other with jokes.
She wears false eyelashes
when she throws herself off the bridge.

JANUARY AFTERNOON, WITH BILLIE HOLIDAY

Her voice shifts as if it were light,
from chalk to parchment to oil.
I think of the sun this morning,
how many knives were flashed
through black, compliant trees;
now she has aged it with her singing,
turned it to milk thinned with water,
a poor people's sun, enough
knowledge to go around.

I want to dance, to bend
as gradually as a flower,
release a ball in slow motion
to follow in the marvelous path
of the unfolding jet streak,
love's expansive finger
across the cheek of the sky:
"Heaven, I'm in heaven . . ."

The foolish old songs were right,
the heart does, actually, ache
from trying to push beyond
itself, this room, the world,
all that can be imagined;
space is not enough space
for its sudden immensity

I am not what you think
This is not what I wanted

Desire has no object, it simply happens,
rises and floats, lighter than air.
But she knows that. Her voice scrapes
against the innocent words of the song!
tomorrow is something she remembers.

IN THE EYE OF THE HURRICANE

We ride in the clearing, the one
incredible patch of blue
in the world's murderous weather

We fly to our next feeding
on dirty money and dirty lungs,
to strawberries in the snow

We ride in our windless blind spot
cushioned by bodies swaddled in flags,
stabilized by disaster

We guess that our bread is enriched
with human bone meal, we suspect
our dentists of melting down wedding rings

We wonder how long they can last,
our charms, our beds to die in,
our bread, before it turns into stone

Shell Form by Norma Dickey (Alaska), from Exxon, U.S.A.'s Salon of Alaskan Artists.
Courtesy: Exxon Company, U.S.A.

THE PRIVATE LIFE

What happens, happens in silence:

The man from New York City
feels himself going insane
and flies to Brazil to rest,

The piano student in Indiana
lovingly gathers the prune pits
Horowitz left on his plate
the only time he ate breakfast there,

My daughter daydreams of marriage
and has suddenly grown
three inches taller than I,

And now, this icy morning,
we find another tree,
an aspen, doubled over,
split in two at the waist:
no message, no suicide note.

       *   *   *

Fruit Market:
age-spotted avocados,
lemons with goose-flesh;
navel oranges,
pears with flushed cheeks;
apples like buttocks,
pineapples like stockades;
coconut heads with instructions:
"Pierce the eyes with an awl,
allowing the milk to run out,
then tap hard with a hammer
until the outer covering cracks—"

life, our violent history,
lies speechless and mild in these bins.

      *   *   *

We are being eaten by words.
My face is smeared with headlines;
my lungs, blue tubes, are always on;
you come home smelling of printer's ink.

The teletype is a dragon's mouth;
ripped out, its tongue grows back
at the speed of sound:

5,000 tons of explosives were dropped
The hijacker wore a business suit
His late model Triumph was found overturned
She said she had taken fertility drugs
The boy stood on the burning deck
The girl's body was found in a cornfield
The President joked with newsmen
The two youths were killed execution-style
The National Safety Council reported
A spokesman for the hospital said
The blond actress disclosed

(Your house is on fire, your children are gone)

Stop it. What happens,
happens in silence:
in a red blood-cell,
a curl in the brain,
in the ignorant ovum,
the switched-on nerves;

it happens in eyes before the scream,
in memory when it boils over,
in the ravine of conscience,
in the smile that says, *come to bed.*

Today—my snow-capped birthday—
our red hibiscus is blooming again.
Months of refusal; now
one sudden silent flower,
one inscrutable life.

AT THE WORLD'S BUSIEST CORNER

State and Madison, Chicago

Blind, black and believing
—archaic trinity—
he fixes burned-out eyes
on an abandoned heaven
as he shouts and chants
his hoarse, relentless gospel:
Put God back in your lives.

Whose god, old man? What you hear
are sounds of summer and money,
as unbelieving waves
spill past you every time
the stop light clicks to green;
whose god, in what disguise?
We carry our gods in our skins,
our wallets, our sons and daughters;
for some of us, angels
stream from the jab of a needle,
for others, infinite mercy
listens beside a couch;
we pray
to the promise of stars and numbers
if we are lonely,
and if we are young, to the smile
that curls in the lotus of flesh;
we pick and choose from among
patented miracles:
shall we be saved by a shiny pill
or a shining vision?

*Once I was blind, but now
I see,* he shouts at us,
at the polluted sky.
His face is rapt, his eyes
are two locked doors.

*Our readers are already acquainted with
Lisel Mueller's work. In addition to her own
books, she has appeared in numerous
anthologies, including* Heartland *and*
Rising Tides.

I MADE NO CHOICE

I decided nothing.

One day you simply appeared in your stupid boat,
your killer's hands, your disjointed body, jagged as a shipwreck,
skinny-ribbed, blue-eyed, scorched, thirsty, the usual,
pretending to be—what? a survivor?

Those who say they want nothing
want everything.
It was not this greed
that offended me, it was the lies.

Nevertheless I gave you
the food you demanded for the journey
you said you planned; but you planned no journey
and we both knew it.

You've forgotten that,
you made the right decision.
You're having a good time here,
the trees bend in the wind, you eat, you rest,
you think of nothing,
your mind, you say,
is like your hands, vacant:

vacant is not innocent.

UNTITLED

We walk in the cedar grove
intending love, no one is here

but the suicides, returned
in the shapes of birds
with their razor-blue
feathers, their beaks like stabs, their eyes
red as the food of the dead, their single
irridescent note,
complaint or warning:

Everything dies, they say,
Everything dies.
Their colours pierce the branches.

Ignore them. Lie on the ground
like this, like the season
which is full and not theirs;

our bodies hurt them,
our mouths tasting of pears, grease,
onions, earth we eat
which was not enough for them,
the pulse under the skin, their eyes
radiate anger, they are thirsty:

Die, they whisper, Die,
their eyes consuming
themselves like stars, impersonal:

they do not care whose
blood fills the sharp trenches
where they were buried, stake through
the heart; as long
as there is blood.

*"I live on a farm in Ontario, raise sheep and
hens, and am about to start another novel . . .
I hope . . .," writes Margaret Atwood, a
renowned Canadian novelist and poet. Her
latest book of poems is* Power Politics, *and
many readers will remember her novels*
The Edible Woman *and* Surfacing.

Palladium by Stella Waitzkin (New York), 1973. Collection of Eleanor Ward. Polyester, resin and wood.

THE TROUBLE WITH WOMEN

by Eleanor Rackow Widmer
Professor, Department of Literature,
University of California-San Diego, La Jolla.

Berger, Thomas, *Regiment of Women.* New York, Simon and Schuster. 1973. $8.95

Owens, Iris, *After Claude.* New York, Farrar, Straus, and Giroux. 1973. $6.95

Consider this vision of the 21st century: Georgie Cornell, a 29 year old "boy" rises in the morning and prepares for his job in a publishing firm; he shaves his face, chest, and calves, dons bikini briefs, bra and pantyhose, a white tailored blouse and a kelly green pleated skirt. Precisely because he knows that he is considered pretty and well-groomed, with eye and face makeup perfect, and silver earrings and bracelets that cannot be faulted, he experiences anxiety as he secures his door with three locks and clutches his purse to his breasts (achieved through plastic prosthesis). Suppose a female mugger or junkie lurks nearby, ready to commit violence at knifepoint? Heroically, Georgie dons his gas mask to combat air pollution, ignores the obscenities of unemployed women who idle in the savage streets, and minces on high heels past the turreted wall across town until a black woman toting a machine gun allows him to enter the inner city of New York.

Though Georgie realizes that black women want white boys for one purpose only, he simpers provocatively for the black guard. Georgie fears all women, including his analyst, Dr. Prine, whom he visits before work. Dr. Prine wears dark trousers and a jacket, a self-adhesive nylon beard, and black horn-rimmed glasses. To combat Georgie's assertion of sexual frigidity, she straps on a dildo, and with Georgie spread-eagled on the table, gives him a treatment. He responds with nothing but pain. Tears flood his eyes at the sense of his worthlessness.

Is this the ultimate in a female writer's revenge? Hardly. It is a novel written by Thomas Berger, *The Regiment of Women,* and it is a disappointing, if clever, satire. In this enclosed and strangely horrifying world, the roles of men and women are totally reversed. It is the women who govern the state, who serve in the army, who police the cities, who wage wars, negotiate laws, and are the arbiters of custom. It is women who are lecherous, self-aggrandizing, bossy, and who brag, boast, and parade the incompetence and fluttery ineffectiveness of men. Mary, rather than Jesus, is the common curse word. For women who violate the laws, the punishment is lobotomy. For men who practice transvestism, that is, dressing in trousers, or sexual perversion, attempting to insert the penis into a female, the punishment is castration. And why should castration be a threat in a world in which the plastic dildo is king and the penis is used for the artificial milking for the Sperm Bank? Because eunuchs lose their looks, and without his looks, what's a boy to do?

At first blush, *Regiment of Women* would appear as a savage dystopia in which the humiliations and oppression experienced by women of the 20th century are foisted on men of the 21st. "Once," a male friend of Georgie's confides in conspiratorial whispers, "men controlled the state." To Georgie Cornell the statement is not merely seditious but questionable. Few have actual knowledge of that time when men did not perform menial tasks, act as "mattresses" for powerful women, or fill their lives with trivia about cosmetics and fashion. More important—and to verify it his male friend produces a pornographic photo of a woman suckling a child—in that long ago era women allegedly bore children. Georgie knows that he was born at a birth facility where he emerged from a stainless steel incubator, and that during the compulsory six months spent in the barracks for the Sperm Term, men have to submit, not just to the humiliation of being milked by machines, but to the repetition of courses in stitchery, embroidery, and flower arrangements. Except for a rare novelist, men are not considered worthy of engaging in the arts, and just as they are personally considered as decorative objects, so are their mild forays into creativity stultified, routinized, limited to embellishing the domestic. Men do not have the genius of women.

But if the reader is temporarily beguiled into seeing Thomas Berger as the ardent champion of the current woman's cause, the illusion is soon destroyed by the unfolding of events. In a series of bizarre episodes, Georgie is arrested for wearing women's clothing, trousers, is imprisoned in a Hall of Detention, and though formerly described as "a good boy" who wishes only to conform slavishly, even to the extent of pandering himself to maintain the job at which he is ludicrously inept, he finds enough courage and cunning to execute a jail break. Subsequently, he becomes the darling of the underground movement that wishes to overthrow the tyranny of women and reestablish the assertiveness of men.

And herein lies the crux of the ambiguity. Berger is so skillful and seductive that the reader cheers when Georgie undergoes surgery to have his breasts removed and to act as an undercover agent at the Sperm Camp. We identify with Georgie; we feel our pulses quicken as he casts off his old role. During an identity crisis at the camp, Georgie, sick of "vulva envy" and the cowardice of his fellow men cries out in despair to the psychiatrist assigned to him:

Women would be just like men if they had a penis and balls. Why don't men play football? Because they might get hit there. And the same goes for boxing and wrestling. Women may be smaller, but they are vulnerable. It's nature's cruel joke to make men the larger and stronger sex and then give them this [a penis] which nullifies everything else.

Who would deny Georgie the right to be prideful, rather than abject, about the staff between his legs, especially in a world where there is no human contact, no lovely, delicious, ecstatic, mind shattering and body renewing fucking as we know it? We delight when Georgie breaks out of camp, taking with him a female FBI agent who, like Georgie, yearns to renounce her imposed slavery.

When Georgie casts off his wig and she claps it on her shorn hair, when Georgie flings off his pantyhose and struggles into trousers while the girl awkwardly adjusts a skirt, when they careen down the highway in an Army truck which she drives because men have been considered too incompetent to handle the wheel, we wish nothing more than their escape. But where and towards what are they heading? Why, beyond their pursuers to an isolated area where they have to hunt and fish to survive, and where, wonder of wonders, they fall to normal copulation—and adore it. Our final view of the hero and heroine is in an untamed Garden of Eden. With the high spirits and the high rod befitting the pioneers in an untamed land, Georgie rolls his mate over so that he is on top.

And he inserted himself this time. If he was going to be builder and killer, he could be boss once in awhile. Also, he was the one with the protuberant organ.

Therefore, what we have experienced in Georgie's pilgrimage is scarcely the break with custom with which the novelist has tantalized us in his opening chapters. While seeming to decry the exploitation of men, that is our women, he is actually leading us back to a situation in which the hero is a "builder," a "killer," a "boss"— and this based on "the protuberant organ."

Revolutionary indeed!

Although Berger's style is lively and he is fiendishly inventive in delineating every aspect of his curious world, his ideology is maddeningly arrested. In dystopian novels of almost half a century ago, such as Zamiatin's *We*, the sensuous life can be found in the green forest beyond the wall; in Huxley's *Brave New World*, the lovers trail off hand in hand into the pastures. No less in *Regiment of Women*. The satire that allegedly espouses the cause of women through the trick mirror of men-cast-as-women ends with the standard, pastoral reflection: the return to the idyllic and sequestered land that denies the regimentation of a mechanized society and reaffirms the verities of the individual couple annealed with the fire of the hot *shtick*. D. H. Lawrence would have nodded in approval. He could not have asked more for Lady Chatterley!

In contrast, the heroine of Iris Owen's brilliantly written novel, *After Claude*, settles for an all too modish solution to the female problem—the last scenes find her masturbating with her cries recorded on tape. Of the two writers, Iris Owens is the more honest. She began her career writing porno in Paris for Girodias of Olympia press. A veteran of four such novels published under the name of Harriet Daimler, *After Claude* bears the imprint of a prestigious New York publishing house.

As a deliberately cultivated in-joke, Ms. Owens uses the name Harriet for her heroine in *After Claude*, thus linking it with the author's own pseudonym. The authenticity of Harriet's character and her curious plight as a victim of cultural shock after a five year sojourn in Paris, strikes the reader as at least partially autobiographical. But to characterize *After Claude* as the inevitable lightly veiled autobiography of a "first" novel is to deny Ms. Owens her due both as a savagely accurate reporter of the current Greenwich Village-Chelsea Hotel scene, and as a gallow humorist of major order. It is not so much what happens in *After Claude* as the way it is said, with biting verve and accuracy for New Yorkese that Mary McCarthy and her reliance on "facts" would well envy.

Through the voice of Harriet, Owens devastates each character with concise irony. Her observation of the hero, "according to

Claude, everyone, with the possible exception of his heroes Mick Jagger and Mao-Tse-tung, was a fag," is no less perceptive than that of Rhoda, the Village ugly, who claims to be "a defender of women's rights, black rights, prisoner's rights, Puerto Rican, gay and Vietnamese rights, when it came to my rights, the good old capitalist line was drawn." Nor does Owens limit herself to Greenwich Village weirdos; she polishes off middle class women with equal aplomb. "Maxine, Jewish mother and wife was fighting off an airtight pair of white shantung hip huggers. Above the carnage, through the transparency of a fishnet polo shirt, you could see a kosher delicatessen. . . . She lit a cigarette with an efficient click of her gold Dupont lighter, her tiny, pointy fingers rigid with wedding bands."

And this same, crisp detail informs the dialogue:

> *"You're the first stewardess I've met socially. . . . Tell me, do you believe that stewardesses and nurses are pathologically promiscuous as a result of their occupations constantly confronting them with death?*
>
> *"Well, I really don't know." She played with her smoked salmon. "Next time you land in a hospital, why don't you ask one of the nurses?"*

Because the style propels the narrative at immense speed, the surface of the book is fairly simple. It opens with Harriet about to be evicted by her lover, a Frenchman in white jeans who works for television. Six months before, Claude literally rescued Harriet from the doorstep of the tenement where her friend, Rhoda-Regina mercilessly and brutally cast her out. Or so says Harriet. Not only does she tell her own story, but through so superior a sensibility as to conceive of her every defect as a virtue. Harriet rarely stirs from bed until noon and then only to watch quiz programs to which she can respond condescendingly. She cooks not, neither does she clean, and rather than boil water for instant coffee— "Who can cook in this heat?"—she repairs to bed with half a gallon of ice cream. Her entire wardrobe cradles on the seat of a rocking chair, and when preparing for an evening's festivities, she wears her tie-dye skirt and Mexican blouse into the shower. After all, aren't they both drip dry?

But Harriet is more than the sum of her eccentricities. A seasoned hypochondriac, Harriet lies supine in Rhoda's apartment for months, with mononucleosis as her excuse, and living with Claude she affects every disease known to woman except paralysis of the tongue. Ah, how acrid Harriet can talk! She has opinions on everything, and nothing can stay her flood. To a movie about Christ she responds by labeling him a "fag," and when Claude demands that she move out, she counters by asking him whether he intends to head the Communist Party and marry a certified virgin of a good family. Trying to seduce Claude before he leaves for work, Harriet quips, "So you'll miss one mugging. Isn't saving our relationship more important?" Harriet resists eviction by stocking up on a survival diet consisting of "fourteen cans of tuna, a half dozen tins of antipasto packed in virgin oil, seven frozen TV turkey dinners, seven frozen deep-fried shrimp dinners, four packages of Hydrox cookies," to assuage her gourmet tastes. She also has her lock changed. To no avail. Claude shows up with a strongman and has her delivered to the Chelsea Hotel.

Up to this point, the novel is one of the most commendable that I have read in years—swift, witty, unsentimental, without a scrap of excess in its conception. The heroine is the victimizer as well as the victim, constant only in her outrageous inconstancies. She clings to anyone who will shelter her with the cloying stamina of a rhesus monkey, but she lashes out at her benefactors with the sting of a venomous snake. Though she advises us that "life is not a quiz show," she demands the right to its prizes. Let those who will work. Doesn't Harriet deserve the prerogative not to when she gives so gloriously of her untidy self?

Her parasitic condition rarely dawns on her. Her motto might well be, "I suffer, therefore I am." And the reader, far from being repelled by her, admires the gusto with which she pursues her mock slavery.

Where the novel breaks down—and alas it does—is in the latter quarter, when Harriet is ensconced in the Hotel Chelsea. Because the landscape is by now familiar, we are led to expect further permutations in this mannered comedy: "It occurred to me that the room was excessively suicide-proof. No bathtub to slash your wrists in. No beams to hang from. The windows were painted shut to discourage the impulsive leaps. A gun would do the job, but that was a man's way."

Inexplicably, Harriet then talks her way into the suite of Roger and his groupies, members of an institute whose men seem to thrive sexually by the vicarious act of listening to the recorded squeals of women giving themselves orgasms, and these women are a mindless, hypnotised, freaked-out lot. Because of the bravado with which Harriet enacts her scenes with Claude, we are not prepared for her to capitulate to Roger, since he is not only repulsive but dangerous. "I recognized in Roger a soul-mate, not to say savior, which is unusual when you consider this childish prejudice I have regarding prematurely balding, soft-skinned, pale-eyed fetus types . . . Let me get the business of Roger's bad teeth out of the way. They tell you that this extraordinarily evolved man has known pain." But pain, or more accurately, captivity, is what Roger inflicts.

With Claude, Harriet is alert, resourceful, endlessly inventive in her combat. But with Roger, an evil character who warns her not to leave her room "except when absolutely necessary," or talk to strangers, or discuss the institute, Harriet is a whimpering, fearful slave. And why? Because Roger has shown her the way to self-orgasms. One would imagine that to a woman of Harriet's sophistication, such release would literally be child's play. Potentially, one can sense the black humor and the intended satire of this twist in Harriet's fate. Except that it's too uncomfortable to be funny. If Ms. Owens wished to satirize Manson and his clan, the notion is antipathetic to comedy.

Like a cliffhanger, the book ends precipitously, with the heroine confined to her room awaiting Roger's return. We pray he never does, and remind ourselves, after the fact, that Harriet will somehow survive. But for the notorious, larger-than-life combatant to be reduced to saying, "It was gratifying to receive orders," and from an impotent creep like Roger, is too close to the sinister for laughter.

An anti-heroine who thumbs her nose at the bourgeois values of cleanliness, a steady job, marriage, and who lives by virtue of her two mouths is one thing; a brainwashed clinging hysteric, metamorphosed from the *momser* of Morton Street to the Charity Case at the Chelsea, is another. Had Iris Owens rested with what she knows from the gut, neither the novel nor its heroine would have floundered. But the concluding episodes not only violate the essential bravery of Harriet, but have the feel of imagined sensationalism, of the old porno hand at its funky work. Still, Harriet, in *After Claude,* is worth your acquaintance, and so is her gifted creator. □

AESTHETIC PURITY OR MIND-RAPE?

by Carole Gottlieb Vopat
Assistant Professor of English, University of Wisconsin-Parkside, Kenosha.

Hess, Thomas B. and Baker, Elizabeth C., eds., *Art and Sexual Politics.* New York, Collier Books, 1973. $1.95.

Hess, Thomas B. and Nochlin, Linda, eds., *Woman as Sex Object.* New York, Art News Annual XXXVIII, 1972. $7.95.

Linda Nochlin, in her keynote essay, "Why Have There Been No Great Women Artists?," does not argue that male and female artists are inherently different, that an artist who is a woman paints in a different style with different perceptions than a man—nor, again, does she deny it; rather, she suggests that such a study has yet to be made. What she is more concerned with is the fact that it is hard to be a woman in this world and survive whole and adult; it is hard particularly to be a woman and something else at the same time—especially an artist.

Art, like everything else, discriminates against women. The answer to the question posed in Nochlin's title is simple and, one would imagine, indisputable: there have been no great women artists because society has been, and still is, sexist. There are several alternative answers: the most popular is that women artists are not as good or as numerous as male artists (no female Michelangelos, no female Rubens) because Women Are Inferior. The idea is never stated quite as baldly as that; after all, we, and especially those of us who muse about matters of art and culture, are a sophisticated and civilized people. But that is what it comes down to; whether the theory derives from biology, sociology, theology, anthropology, or psychology, the meaning is the same: woman is by nature stupid, or limited, or uncreative. And yet the truth is not far off. Of course, women are not by nature stupid; they are by nature human beings. But they are by nurture, by training, by culture, by environment, taught to be stupid. We live in a society in which true and enduring artistic achievement, the artistic life itself, is not lady-like, and the tyranny of what is lady-like has only recently been mitigated.

One half of our population has been and still is raised in such a way that there can be no geniuses among us. One of the primary prerequisites of the artist, more primary than talent or discipline, is a self, an "I," and with that "I," that inherent right of saying "me!" and having it mean something, comes a sense of power and, more important, of authority. Without it there can be no great art, no art at all; and there has not been.

Women have always dreamed dreams and seen visions. But the confidence as well as the professional training to set those dreams and visions down, to make the children of their imagination as sturdy as the children of their body, that has been bred out of them. Women have not taken their insights seriously; they spend them over coffee, sigh

157

them out scrubbing the floor, and when they think of the artist's life, which means privacy, and a right to time, space and training, access to materials and the world beyond the home, they envision the disruption of their family, their husband's anger, their children's whines, and it doesn't seem worth it. For women, unlike men, do not have a tradition of artistic rebellion or romantic pariahdom behind them. Few of us run off to Tahiti; who would look after the children?

Women have no tradition save the one of passivity and submission decreed for us by male society. We have been robbed of our history and of our artists, those who speak for us, to us, who give us back our lives ordered, meaningful, sometimes heightened, burnished, even beautiful. As far as women are concerned, creativity has been more a problem than a gift. The traits that define creativity—the independence, the curiosity, the initiative, the unwillingness to conform, the self-esteem, as well as the great amounts of discipline, the absorption and concentration to the exclusion of all else— these very traits are bred out of women, are "unladylike," "masculine," encouraged in little boys but repressed in little girls, whose primary responsibilities will be to men and not to themselves. Many women grow up to play at art rather than to devote their lives to it; they satisfy their restless energy and their guilt with Sunday painting and dilettantism, rather than with serious and disciplined art.

It is naive to believe that if a woman in the past had had "True Genius" she would have been able to transcend the limitations placed on her by birth and training to pro-

Untitled—1969. Photo by Anne Noggle (Albuquerque, NM).

duce work of such blinding quality it and she would have had to have been recognized. Even if we accept for a moment, as Nochlin does not, the myth of the genius, it is also true, as Simone de Beauvoir points out, that geniuses are not only born, they are made; genius needs a social and psychological environment conducive to its development. It *is* a myth that genius develops in a vacuum, on a hillside or in a cave. Genius can be strangled, it can be repressed, it can turn against itself in guilt, anger and frustration; without training, without literacy, without money or independence, without encouragement or an audience, genius can die, or, worse, its creative passions become self-destructive; not art but insanity, suicide, murder.

Linda Nochlin proves with concrete historical example this frightening truth about women: that society is joined as it were in an unconscious conspiracy to keep woman out of the studio, the museum, the gallery, the university, as she has systematically been kept out of any of the forums of power or achievement. That it is no accident of birth or defect of genes that we have no great women artists, but the result of a steadily applied program, a System, an Establishment, of rules and roles; that it is a white male world and has been; our art, as her second book of essays, *Woman As Sex Object,* clearly illustrates, is white male art for white male audiences, made up of white male images and fantasies.

What must then be studied when one studies art history is not the biography of the individual artist, but rather the society in which the artist lived, a society whose power and influence cannot be denied by any theory

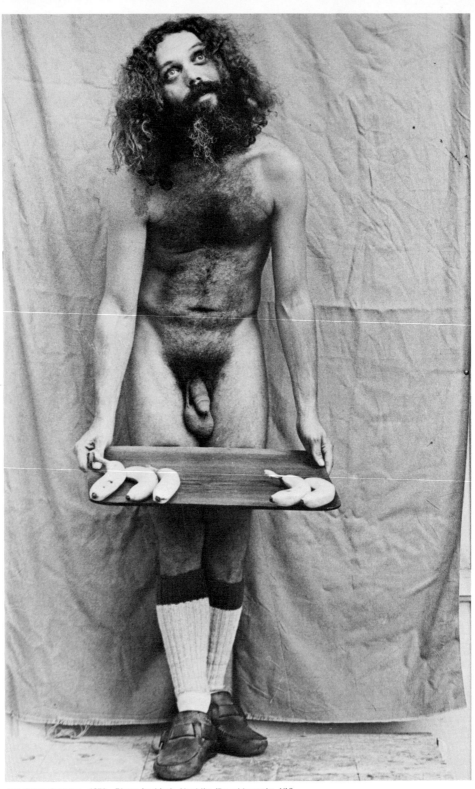

Buy Some Bananas, 1972. Photo by Linda Nochlin (Poughkeepsie, NY).

of genius or superhuman transcendent individuality. Concluding that "the conditions for producing art" are more important than the study of "genius," Nochlin studies those conditions to prove that society has prevented women from making art, by undermining their confidence in general and, more pragmatically, by denying them access to training, encouragement, and, even more basically, to the tools of their trade: until just recently in art history, women artists were not allowed public access to the nude body; a woman could pose for the picture she was not allowed to paint, or, often, to look at.

It is ironic that a study of the erotic in art can be entitled *Woman as Sex Object* and make perfect sense, for erotic art *means* erotic-for-men. Images of women in art are what one might expect: variations on the madonna-whore syndrome. Yet the nudes and vampires are for the most part passive, still; they look stolidly out at the viewer or gaze solemnly if languidly into mirrors; these are not studies of woman's sensuality and sexuality, but of the sexuality of the male viewer. Even today there is no vocabulary, no fund of images, for women to express their own erotic fantasies. Our culture does not present males as sex objects; society's image of man is just the opposite of the odalisque and sloe-eyed bather. Rather, it is one of power, possession and domination; swords, spears, lances. To be the object of a sex fantasy, one must be an object, and men do not fit easily, publicly, into that role. There is no tradition of male passivity, male voluptuousness or availability, nor are there welcoming sensual images of penises; lance is too painful, while banana, which Nochlin suggests, is ludicrous. Clearly a new language will have to be formulated, in cinema, in literature, as well as in art, new metaphors and images to express the woman artist's and the woman viewer's sexuality.

As such studies make clear, Art to Nochlin is not "the direct, personal expression of individual emotional experience," but rather "involves a self-consistent language of form, more or less dependent upon, or free from, given temporarily-defined conventions, schemata, or systems of notation, which have to be learned or worked out, through study, apprenticeship, or a long period of individual experimentation." Art is not personal but social. Rosa Bonheur, for example, succeeded not only because she was good, but because, Ms. Nochlin points out, the institution of art was changing in such a way as to admit and recognize her. With the rise of the middle class as patrons rather than the aristocracy, smaller paintings, generally of everyday subjects rather than great mythological or religious scenes, came into demand; animal painting became popular, and Bonheur, who was denied access to other outlets but who could, indeed, look upon naked animals without risking much, was its most accomplished, successful practitioner. A "tomboy" as a child who witnessed her martyr mother's decline from overwork and poverty, Bonheur never married and, encouraged early by her drawingmaster father, dedicated herself to her art. Yet at the same time that she rejected the conventional feminine role of her times, cropped her hair, lived with a woman companion, habitually wore men's attire, she felt compelled to justify her rejection not as protest or symbol but in terms of practicality, and to count herself an exception. Concludes Nochlin, "it is somewhat pathetic that this highly successful world-renowned artist . . . should feel compelled late in life to justify and qualify her perfectly reasonable assumption of masculine ways, for any reason whatsoever; it is more pathetic still that she should feel compelled to attack her less modest, trouser-wearing sisters. Yet her conscience, despite her supportive father and worldly success, still condemned her for not being a 'feminine' woman."

The fault, Nochlin asserts, "lies not in our stars, our hormones, our menstrual cycles, or our empty internal spaces, but in our institutions and our education—education understood to include everything that happens to us from the moment we enter, head first, into this world of meaningful symbols, signs and signals." She calls upon women to "face up to the reality of their history and of their present situation"; to reject the glamour of the underdog, the token, and the outsider and, instead, "at the same time that they destroy false consciousness, take part in the creation of institutions in which clear thought and true greatness are challenges open to anyone—man or woman—courageous enough to take the necessary risk."

For if the fault has been with the institution, it is the institution which must be changed. It is no longer and, in fact, has never been, a matter of an individual "raising her consciousness," gaining personal confidence and courage; nor is it a simple question of persuading men, politely or violently, to let us into the world. Society itself and the institutions it supports and creates must change; nothing less than a revolution—if bloodless, if "decent," a revolution nonetheless, for all that it must take place in the heightened self-conscious world of culture and civilization, in the museums and galleries rather than in the streets. And the idea of the "one-woman revolution" is as romantic as that of "the true genius"; collectivity, society, institutions, cannot be fought with individuality; it is sentiment to believe that one pure heart can change the destiny of millions, or of one other, or even of oneself.

Where Linda Nochlin presents an historical view of woman's position in the art institution, Elizabeth C. Baker and Lee Hall bring us up to date on women in the arts. Asserting that for all baby's come a long way, "there is still serious discrimination against the woman artist" which prevents many women from sustaining, let alone attempting, productive and successful careers, Elizabeth C. Baker in her essay "Sexual Art-Politics," points out the isolation in which a woman artist must work, the subtle and not so subtle doubts about her quality and her seriousness, the assumption that of a married pair, artists or otherwise, it is the male who has the "real" career. Although no longer cut off automatically from essential professional training, the woman art student is rarely taken seriously nor is she encouraged to pursue a "real" career; rather it is assumed she is merely dabbling until she finds a man. After she leaves art school, neither grants nor teaching appointments come her way; those that are offered to her are usually fewer hours for fewer pay at tasks that have less and less relation to her actual artistic interests. Although "great art has no sex," dealers are reluctant to show more than a small minority of women artists, while other galleries, whether by design or not, exclude them entirely. Museums are less ready to support young women artists, less willing to take a chance or grant them benefit of the doubt; a woman must be famous *before* she is given private showings or added to collections. Women who have succeeded despite this discrimination are exceptions. Nor do women critics or dealers themselves rush to champion women artists, as the women artists themselves tend to refuse to help or encourage each other. As whites once feared the epithet of "nigger-lover," so women in the arts shun or in the least are ambivalent to their own sex; women who have "made it" in this man's media are reluctant to dilute any of their specialness. Although Baker hastens to reassure them that "a conscious attempt to be even handed need in no way carry implications of diluted critical standards," by waving the banner of "aesthetic purity" women themselves, like the men they copy, can ignore justice without guilt.

Lee Hall, Chairperson of the Art Department at Drew University, is quick to assert in her essay, "In the University," that her own academic success is not typical. The university remains that part of society which, under guise of independent and fearless inquiry, of the academic freedom to disagree and scrutinize, manages yet to affirm with logic and data those very ideas the rest of society accepts on blind faith. It is no surprise, then, that the position of women in the university mirrors that of women in society as a whole. There are fewer women on academic faculties; men are rewarded better; men have more political power in terms of shaping policies and priorities; women are clustered in the lower ranks; few women govern or administrate; and all women are pursued by myths of their emotional instability, their periodic moodiness, their frivolousness, their irrationality and their irresponsibility. Water wears away rocks; the sheer mundane weight of these prejudices can in time force an ambitious woman into passivity, anxiety, apathy and guilt, can erode her self confidence and cause her to set limits to her own expectations and achievements.

Despite the wealth of reasoned evidence by Nochlin, Hess, Baker and Hall, the ten women artists called upon to respond to Nochlin's article ("Why Have There Been No Great Women Artists? Ten Replies") are most of them negative, if not actually hostile. Arranged in descending order of animosity, the artists are primarily threatened by Nochlin's emphasis on art as social rather than personal, and on the artist as product of time and place rather than as individual genius beyond history. With their rejection of art as social comes a rejection and a fear of the political itself, a quick denial that art as well as the art world surrounding it has to do with the mundane and unaesthetic facts of power. Caught in a conflict between their creative responsibilities to themselves as artists and their social responsibilities to themselves as women, these artists have promoted the first to deny the second, despite their admission that for all their aesthetic chastity women are discriminated against in galleries, museums, schools and universities. To view art as political, they argue, is to reduce it to propaganda; to call the artist social is to diminish the self. Let us not debate that now; the problem facing women is one of discrimination, and discrimination is political: it is the tool of supremacy, of control, of domination, of one class by another. It is a class problem, not a personal one. One does not gain power by ignoring it in the name of an exclusive and, in practice, elusive, individuality.

But individuality is what they are promoting, and, ultimately, defending. Their vehemence is a measure of their fear: fear of surrendering a hard-earned self importance; fear of admitting responsibility to anything beyond the carefully defined and limited self; fear of collective action and of political consciousness, of working in concert with other women to change the institutions of the art world and of society itself; ultimately, a fear of moving beyond the personal domain, which they have learned somewhat to control, in which one is responsible solely to oneself and one's art, a manageable, self-willed world, into the larger and more threatening arena of the social and the political, wherein one is responsible for other people, for history, humankind, the way things are and will be. Their remarks, coming as they do in reaction to threat rather than in response to reason and intellect, force them into awkward stances which reason is quick to overthrow.

Elaine de Kooning and Rosalyn Drexler ("Dialogue") are the most hostile, their remarks scalded with sarcasm. Rather than refute Nochlin, they ridicule her, dismissing her arguments not with proof but with coyly arch role-playing. For example, of the idea, which so incenses them, that art is an institution, they offer only the following: "Institution to me means the Pentagon, the CIA.... Well the point is, I don't want to create any other institutions. I don't want to be *in* an institution." Their conclusions do not support analysis. "Any artist no matter what his [sic] gifts, faces neglect." True, but men artists are not neglected because they are men. "You can't argue with someone's taste." True, but women are excluded from galleries and museums not on the basis of taste but because of sex. "There's no such thing as equality in the arts." True, if one means equal potential or equal value; but all artists ought to have equal opportunity and equal rights.

Often they are self-contradictory. "Well, I think the status quo in the arts is fine as it is . . . , women have exactly the same chance men do . . . . There are no obstacles in the way of a woman becoming a painter or sculptor, other than the usual obstacles that an artist has to face." A second later, de Kooning opines, "There's no doubt, in terms of the numbers of women painters in this country, that women are not bought by collectors to the same extent that men are . . . . They're not exhibited as adequately in museums, are not given teaching posts in the universities." On the one hand, "the question we're discussing is not recognition; the question is the idea of being an artist," yet "I think what can make an artist stop is total neglect."

Tinged with their denials of discrimination is their contempt for their own sex; the oppressed class is blamed for its own oppression: women are the victims not of an established historical program of sexism but of their own weakness; they are not oppressed, only a little neurotic: "Women have had the vote for over fifty years. Where are the women in elective office? Women could have put them there. Who needs to grant what to whom?"

Their vehement individuality forces them into some strange contortions. Being a woman, asserts de Kooning, is totally irrelevant to her art; "we're artists who happen to be women or men among other things we happen to be—tall, short, blonde, dark . . . ." It is debatable whether one's sex is as irrelevant as one's hair color; surely no one would argue any longer that in America one's skin color is "in no way relevant to our being artists." Their assertion that the individual exists independent of society and of sex is naive to say the least; they hold just that romantic view of the artist which Nochlin debunks: "The artist stands for everything against institutions." So great in fact is their need to assert the self, that they conclude that rather than being influenced by history or society, the artist creates his/her own history, the whole world becomes ME: ". . . artists are always choosing their history from day to day and their history follows them as much as it precedes them." Do these women live in some studio in Arcadia, some shepherd's pastorale beyond which nothing exists, no world, no society, no audience, no history, nothing save clouds, canvas and woolly sheep?

Their stance is more extreme than most, yet typical of the resistances offered Nochlin's argument. Artist Bridget Riley ("The Hermaphrodite") solves the question of discrimination quite neatly; calling the artist an "hermaphrodite," and pointing out that while women suffer as women, men also "suffer as men" (with "analogous sociological problems of one sort or another: . . . poverty, unsympathetic marriages, alcoholism," none of which, however, are sex related), she is free to conclude that "women's liberation when applied to artists seems to me to be a naive concept." One surmounts the fact of discrimination by denying not discrimination but sex! Louise Nevelson on the other hand ("Do Your Work") is able to dismiss discrimination by stating categorically that it "should not" exist; nothing exists save the artist and his/her art: "society, personalities, and problems are quite another story." One circumvents the fact of social discrimination by denying not only discrimination but the existence of society itself!

Artist Suzi Gablik ("The Double-Bind") admits that serious discrimination exists but believes that through personal awareness and personal consciousness, a woman can conquer all to become master of her fate and captain of her soul; those women who are less than they want to be are themselves responsible for what she would deem their weakness. She comments on what she calls "the collusion which women often practice" by sacrificing identity for security, as though such self-mutilation were deliberately, consciously willed. The social and political are metamorphosed into the existential; the basic question for Gablik, as for others, becomes: how much can women control? how much is oneself, how much socialization? how much is a human being the product of environment and culture, and how much one's own creation, one's own existential, self-willed Self? To what extent may we be said to be responsible for our destinies? That there have been few women artists up to now suggests overwhelmingly either that women are by nature weak or that the job done on them by society and its deputies has been overpowering. One cannot "will away" discrimination; it is not a personal problem. For Gablik, the answer lies in "reflective self-awareness"; like her counterparts, she runs from the fact of action, politics or group protest. One need only sweep one's head clean and get on with the business of making art, as though, say, one white person clearing his or her heart of bigotry and mistrust does anything to ease the despair and destitution of hundreds of Blacks, or even of one. One woman artist's success does not cancel out a history of discrimination or the real presence today of a noxious prejudice that stops a hundred women for every one who breaks through. And rather than celebrate the personal strength of the one who breaks through, as do these artists, who themselves broke through, we must instead act, change, and revolutionize, must celebrate not individual genius but collective strength.

In their fervor to defend themselves, most of the responding artists distort Nochlin's ideas, contradict their own, are flip or arch or rhetorical, anything but concrete. Statistics and injustices are brushed aside or relegated to the past as these artists insist upon their individuality, asserting their romantic but naive and ultimately selfish credo: I am not a woman, I am ME; my responsibilities are to myself and my art. None offers facts, none refers to incidents in her own life, using the personal to refute Nochlin's historical lessons; rather, there is only the wispy belief that denying discrimination loudly enough will make it disappear, denying the world beyond the studio will render that world, that society, impotent to hurt, thwart and destroy. Most of them, in fact, rather than respond to Nochlin directly, argue against discrimination itself; discrimination *ought not* to exist, we *ought not* to be categorized, we *ought not* to be regarded primarily as women. True enough, but what has *ought* to do with *is*? Art *is* social and political; women *are* categorized and discriminated against; all the bravado in the world will not undo that simple and tragic fact.

Perhaps it is because these artists, as women, have had to fight so fiercely to give themselves an "I," a self, to counteract the influence of society upon them, that they resist what they interpret as an attempt to degrade that self and that struggle. Perhaps as artist Marjorie Strider ("Moving Out, Moving Up") compassionately points out, denying the world is the only way to keep on working, for to admit the fact of discrimination is to feel the self-crushing weight of hopelessness, despair, futility and doubt; only very recently has she herself been able to move "from ignoring the facts so you can do your work to being able to admit them and still come through."

Self-protection or selfishness or vanity or fear or naivete or sentiment, and all the while more women are dying, dying from a lack of self, from a lack of encouragement, of a friendly environment in which to grow and become, dying at the hands of media, teachers, counselors, parents, each day more afraid to express a self that daily diminishes like water in a pond drying slowly in from the edge. ☐

TOO MUCH OF A GOOD THING?

by R. E. Sebenthall
Poet and detective novelist.

Chester, Laura and Barba, Sharon, eds., *Rising Tides: 20th Century American Poets.* New York, Washington Square Press. $1.95.

Howe, Florence and Bass, Ellen, eds., *No More Masks!: An Anthology of Poems by Women.* New York, Anchor Press/ Doubleday Anchor Books. $3.95.

As a woman, a feminist and a poet, I find many good things to say of these two anthologies. Both range as far back as Bogan, Wylie, H. D. and Moore. *Rising Tides* includes most of today's better-known women poets as well as a fair sampling of younger ones who are new to me. (If you miss a few prominent names it is because these poets preferred not to appear in an all-woman anthology, or just possibly were writing about other things than being a woman). *No More Masks!* offers by far the most generous helping of the very young and the black. Perhaps as a result of this, it seems the more militantly feminist of the two books. Almost nowhere in either book do the poems fall below a high level of competence; many are excellent poems by any standard. It is obvious (if you doubted it) that yes, Virginia, women can and do write fine poetry.

The editors of both collections state frankly that they sought poems concerned with "what it means to be a woman." That they have been ninety-nine percent successful in this search is evident. Few, if any of the poems, stray beyond this single theme. Blood, babies, delivery rooms and gynecologists abound; one sees that a woman's world today is apparently as dominated by lovers, husbands, fathers, difficult mothers and constricted childhoods, as it ever was. In the introduction to *Rising Tides* Anais Nin writes: "The fusion here is the voice of woman. Woman determined to end woman's mysteries and secrets. We need to know her." This is an admirable aim, but one that can result in too much of a good thing. For by the time we have finished either or both of these books we know her almost too well; we are sated with her; and if there is a single secret left I can't imagine what it would be.

Which brings me to what I feel is wrong with collections like these. Women talking endlessly about what it is to be a woman, preoccupied exclusively with their age-old biological and social problems, even if in fresh terms, do not really widen their horizons. And widening horizons is, as I understand it, the whole purpose of women's liberation. It should be granted, of course, that women exploring themselves with a new frankness and honesty represents a beginning, a stage through which the process of liberation must pass. But we have had a great deal of it, and the question that ought to be asked now is whether that stage hasn't accomplished its purpose, whether or not it isn't time for women to conclude the navel-gazing and step out of doors for a look at the new horizons.

There is another demerit to chalk up against anthologies of this kind. In placing the emphasis on woman's traditional experience, the editors have often selected poems that do not represent the poet's best work. For example, both books offer Moore's "Marriage"—a shrewd dry look at that institution, but a poem that is far from Moore at her incandescent best. Wylie's finest poem "The Eagle and the Mole" is omitted in favor of minor womanly pieces. With the exception of the searing "Daddy," none of Plath's major poems are included. I could multiply such examples. In addition, several poets have told me they wish they might have been represented by stronger, less "woman-oriented" poems, and I must assume there are others here who share that feeling. To this extent then these books do the woman's cause some disservice. They give us women grinding away relentlessly at "what it is to be a woman" rather than women writing the very best poetry of which they are capable. Worse, they suggest something I find it hard to accept: that even after all the liberation flak, women really aren't concerned with anything but men, marriage and motherhood.

I am aware that these remarks could be construed as a plea for women to "write like a man"—whatever that ambiguous phrase may mean. If it means to write well about something besides one's personal life, then I do, indeed, urge women to take that formidable risk. But if it is, as I feel, a ridiculous and meaningless phrase, then I

suggest we toss it out the window and get on with writing well about the thousand and one other things that might fruitfully engage the minds it has now been conceded we do possess. Moore did marvelous things with a jerboa, with a frigate bird and a steam roller, with an endless variety of subjects that had nothing at all to do with being a woman, yet wrote with a consummate skill and brilliance that had nothing at all to do with being a man. The same could be said of many other women poets, including such a major figure as Bishop (conspicuously absent in both books).

Relative to this, one of the editors of No More Masks! bewails the fact that Moore wrote no "confessional poems," never made herself the subject of her work—as if this were some sort of high artistic crime. This attitude apparently fails to understand that a writer's personality or animus flavors every word he or she writes, regardless of what the subject matter may be, regardless of whether or not the writer has dipped into his or her personal life.

One other point might be noted here. Woman's new frankness about herself, especially about her sexual experience, is still enough of a novelty to appeal to the canny editor. Selling poetry is difficult at best; larded with four-letter words and sexual explicitness it becomes a bit more marketable. Both some editors and some women poets seem to be capitalizing on this fact, the women apparently failing to see that in doing so they are going along with their own current beté noire: sexual exploitation.

Finally, granting that most women, contrary to the fears of the doom-sayers, will continue to rock the cradle and keep the home-fires burning, I, for one, see no reason why they should continue to write about nothing else. It seems to me they have thoroughly explored themselves and their problems. I feel it is time they went to the windows now before they picked up their pens. Only if they do so, can we look forward to poems and books in which they will turn their skills and sensibilities to an exploration of that wider world, those new horizons they have struggled so long and arduously to achieve. □

Window #3 Ascension by Roberta Allen (New York), 1971. Window, mirror, wooden balls. 41″ x 22″ x 6″.

STAFF AND PARTICIPANTS OF THE NATIONAL CONFERENCE ON WOMEN AND THE ARTS

September 13-15, 1973
Held at Wingspread, The Johnson Foundation Conference Center, Racine, Wisconsin. Sponsored by the University of Wisconsin-Extension in cooperation with The Johnson Foundation.

Other cooperating agencies: The Wisconsin Arts Council, The Wisconsin Academy of Sciences, Arts and Letters, The Wisconsin Governor's Commission on the Status of Women, and The Wisconsin State Historical Society.

Perry Miller Adato   Workshop Discussion Leader
   Producer and Director, WNET Channel 13, New York.

Marytha Allen
   Chairman, Department of Art, Felician College.

Vivienne Anderson
   Director, Division of Humanities and Arts, The State Education Department, The University of the State of New York.

Dorothy Austin   Workshop Rapporteur
   Writer, *The Milwaukee Sentinel.*

Audrey Baird
   Volunteer Leader and Patron, Wisconsin.

*Frances Bedford   Planning Committee Member
   Assistant Professor of Music, The University of Wisconsin-Parkside.

Marjorie Bitker   Conference Reporter
   Writer, Milwaukee.

Ludmilla Bollow
   Playwright, Milwaukee.

Patricia Burnett
   Painter; Member of Board of Directors, National Organization for Women.

Bonnie Cashin
   Designer, New York.

*Susan Certo   Planning Committee Member and Workshop Rapporteur
   Administrative Secretary, Wisconsin Arts Council.

Helen Chapman
   Past President, General Federation of Women's Clubs, Wisconsin.

*Grace P. Chatterton   Planning Committee Member
   Specialist, The University of Wisconsin-Extension Arts.

Kathryn F. Clarenbach   Conference Consultant and Author of Conference Position Paper
   Founder, National Organization for Women; First President, Interstate Commission on the Status of Women; Professor, University of Wisconsin-Extension.

*Pat Clark   Planning Committee Member and Workshop Rapporteur
   Chairman, Department of Art, The University of Wisconsin-River Falls.

Barbara Coffman
   Associate Curator, Milwaukee Arts Center.

*Karen Cowan   Planning Committee Member
   Dancer; Specialist, The University of Wisconsin-Extension.

Jean Cronon
   Community Arts Organizer, Madison.

Betsy Damon
   Founder, Feminist Art Studio, Ithaca, New York.

Ann Day
   Education Director, Waterloo Recreation and Arts Center, Waterloo, Iowa.

Agnes Denes   Workshop Discussion Leader
   Artist, New York.

Sister Mary Austin Doherty   Workshop Discussion Leader and Rapporteur.
   Professor of Psychology, Alverno College.

Harriet FeBland
   Painter; Vice President, Artist's Equity; Director, Advanced Painters Workshop.

Nathan Feinsinger
   Professor of Law, Center for Teaching and Research in Dispute Settlement, The University of Wisconsin-Madison.

Doris C. Freedman   Workshop Discussion Leader
   President, City Walls, Inc., New York.

Shelbe Freeman
   Administrator and Performing Arts Director, Bronx Council on the Arts; Coordinator, First Congress on Blacks in Dance.

Rita Goodman Conference Coordinator
Program Executive, The Johnson Foundation.

Grace Glueck Speaker
Arts Correspondent and Assistant Metropolitan Editor, *The New York Times.*

*****Gretchen Grimm** Planning Committee Member and Workshop Discussion Leader
Chairman, Department of Art, The University of Wisconsin-Eau Claire.

*****Lorraine Gross** Planning Committee Member and Workshop Rapporteur
Associate Dean, College of Arts, The University of Wisconsin-Whitewater.

William J. Hanford
Dean, College of Fine Arts, The University of Wisconsin-Stevens Point.

Linda Heddle Conference Co-Chairperson
Art Editor, *Arts in Society.*

Ravenna Helson Speaker
Professor of Psycholgy and Research, Institute of Personality Assessment and Research, University of California-Berkeley.

Gertrude B. Herman Workshop Discussion Leader
Associate Professor, Library Science, The University of Wisconsin-Madison.

Fannie Hicklin Speaker
Professor of Theatre, The University of Wisconsin-Whitewater; Director, Readers' Theatre.

*****Mary Hovind** Planning Committee Member
Slide Librarian, Applied Arts Building, The University of Wisconsin-Stout.

Elizabeth Janeway Speaker
Author and critic, New York.

Monika Jensen Conference Co-Chairperson
Associate Editor, *Arts in Society.*

*****Kay Johnson** Planning Committee Member and Workshop Rapporteur
Assistant Director, Center for Theatre Research, The University of Wisconsin-Madison.

Edward Kamarck
Editor, *Arts in Society.*

Frances Kinne (in absentia)
Dean, College of Fine Arts, Jacksonville University.

*****Nancy Knaak** Planning Committee Member and Workshop Coordinator
Professor of Psychology and Dean of Women, The University of Wisconsin-River Falls.

*****Ilona Kombrink** Planning Committee Member and Workshop Rapporteur
Singer; Professor of Voice, The University of Wisconsin-Madison.

Marjorie Kreilick
Artist; Professor of Art, The University of Wisconsin-Madison.

*****Gloria Link** Planning Committee Member
Professor, Speech Department, The University of Wisconsin-Oshkosh.

Valentina Litvinoff
Dance Critic; Choreographer for "Trojan Women," New York.

Margaret E. Mahoney Workshop Discussion Leader
Vice President, Robert Wood Johnson Foundation, New Jersey.

*****Barbara Manger** Planning Committee Member and Workshop Discussion Leader
Artist, Milwaukee.

Kay Mauer Conference Coordinator
Administrative Secretary, The Johnson Foundation.

Mary McCoy
Editorial Secretary, *Arts in Society.*

*****Roberta Mayer** Planning Committee Member
Artist and art instructor, Madison Area Technical College.

*****Mary Michie** Planning Committee Member
Sculptor; Specialist, The University of Wisconsin-Extension.

*****Ruth Milofsky** Planning Committee Member
Artist; Professor, Department of Art, The University of Wisconsin-Milwaukee.

Ruth Mondschein
Special Assistant to the Federal Women's Program, United States Civil Service Commission, Washington.

Harold Montross
Dean, Human and Professional Development, The University of Wisconsin-Extension.

Elvie Moore
Playwright; Associated with the Communicative Arts Academy in Los Angeles.

Charlotte Moser
Library Consultant on Arts and Teacher of Art History, Houston.

*****Eileen Muth** Planning Committee Member
Dancer; Dance Instructor, Department of Physical Education, The University of Wisconsin-LaCrosse.

Anna Nassif
Choreographer; Professor of Dance, The University of Wisconsin-Madison.

Linda Nochlin Speaker
Author; Professor of Art History, Vassar College.

Leslie Paffrath
President, The Johnson Foundation.

Betty Pekul
President, Homemakers Arts Council, Wisconsin.

Lois Jones Pierre-Noel Workshop Discussion Leader
Artist; Professor, Department of Art, Howard University.

Cynthia Pitts Workshop Discussion Leader
Director, Training and Technical Assistance, Community Relations-Social Development Commission, Milwaukee.

Margaret Rahill Workshop Rapporteur
Curator, Charles Allis Art Library, Milwaukee.

Linda Rich
Photographer, Graduate Student in Art, University of Wisconsin-Madison.

Faith Ringgold
Artist; Founder and Member, Women Students and Artists for Black Artist Liberation, New York.

Wilma D. Ringstrom
Playwright; Co-Founder, Midwest Council for Drama and Other Arts, Inc.; Co-Chairman, Department of Fine Arts, Missouri Council of Churches, St. Louis.

Allyn Roberts Workshop Discussion Leader
Psychologist and Author; Head, Midwestern Psychological Services, Madison.

Vera Mowry Roberts
President, American Theatre Association; Chairman, Department of Theatre and Cinema, Hunter College.

Eleanor J. Roe
Lecturer of Law, The University of Wisconsin-Madison.

Patricia Kerr Ross
Associate for the Arts, Office of Vice Chancellor for Academic Programs, State University of New York, Albany.

Barry Schwartz Workshop Rapporteur
Author and critic, Riverside, California.

Gerti H. Sennett
Poet, Writer, and Lecturer; Currently working on history of Menominee Indians, Wisconsin.

*Joan Severa Planning Committee Member
Curator, Wisconsin State Historical Society, Madison.

Theodore Shannon
Director, Human Resources Development, The University of Wisconsin-Extension.

Rose Slivka
Editor, *Craft Horizons*.

Ann Snitau
Professor, English Literature and Women's Studies, Rutgers University.

Clare Spark-Loeb
Associate Director of Drama and Literature, Pacifica KPFK-FM, North Hollywood, California.

Athena Tacha Spear
Artist; Professor, Department of Art, Oberlin College.

Sister Helena Steffens-Meier
Artist-in-Residence, Alverno College.

May Stevens Workshop Discussion Leader
Artist and Lecturer, New York.

Adolph Suppan
Dean, School of Fine Arts, The University of Wisconsin-Milwaukee.

Lenore Sweet
Community Organizer, Lac du Flambeau, Wisconsin.

May Natalie Tabak
Author and critic, New York.

Rita W. Tallent
Assistant to the Chancellor, The University of Wisconsin-Parkside.

Evelyn Terry
Printmaker, Milwaukee.

Ruth Thomas
English Teacher, Washington High School, Milwaukee.

Lois Wagner
Student in Business Administration and Music, The University of Wisconsin-Parkside.

Jeanne Weber
Specialist, Public Information, The University of Wisconsin-Extension.

Lee Weiss
Artist, Madison.

*Marjorie Whitsitt Planning Committee Member
Professor, Department of Art, The University of Wisconsin-Superior.

PAST ISSUES

Available on microfilm from:
University Library Services
Xerox Corporation
Ann Arbor, Michigan 48106

Printed Volumes 1-3 available from:
Johnson Reprint Corporation
111 Fifth Avenue
New York, New York 10003

Clothbound set $57.50
Paperbound set $50.00
Per vol., paper $17.50

INDEXING AND LISTING

Arts in Society is indexed in:
Abstracts of English Studies
Annual International Bibliography of the Modern Language Association of America
Annual Bibliography of the Modern Humanities Research Association
Art Bibliographies (England)
Bibliographische Zeitschrift für Asthetik (Germany)
Current Contents, Education
Current Index to Journals in Education
Dictionnaire International Des Literatures Parallelles
Directory of Scholarly and Research Publishing Opportunities
Index to Little Magazines
Keylines
Magazines for Libraries
Modern Language Association Abstract System
Music Article Guide
Public Affairs Information Service Bulletin
Review of Reviews
Rilm Abstracts of Music Literature
Sociological Abstracts, Inc.
Western Psychological Services

Arts in Society is listed in:
Academic Media
Alberto Andreozzi Editore (Italy)
Directory of Scholastic Publications in the Humanities
Literary Marketplace
The Standard Periodical Directory
The Writer
Ulrich's International Periodical Directory
Writers' and Artists' Yearbook (London, England)

BOOKSTORE DISTRIBUTION

National Distribution to the Bookstore Trade:
B. DeBoer
188 High Street
Nutley, New Jersey 07110

Subscription and Bookstore Distribution for Great Britain and Europe:
B. F. Stevens and Brown, Ltd.
Ardon House, Mill Lane
Godalming, Surrey,
England.

ARTS IN SOCIETY
INSTRUCTIONAL RESOURCE PACKAGES

Relevant topics from *Arts in Society* are now translated into multi-media for easy use in high schools, colleges, and adult groups. Tapes, slides, posters, articles, and bibliographies are organized into attractive and easy-to-handle packages. Send for more information or order them now on the attached order form.

Art and Technology:
Includes 80 slides of Op, Minimal, Kinetic and Light Art; a 12-minute taped narration; articles on the topic; four 12" x 18" posters; and a teacher's study guide.

Art and Environment:
Includes 80 slides on the "New Realism" in art, Pop art, the Bauhaus, Frank Lloyd Wright and other visuals of the environment; a 12-minute taped narration; articles on the topic; four 12" x 18" posters; and a teacher's study guide.

Art and Social Revolution:
Includes 80 slides of Daumier, Goya, Picasso, Rauschenberg, Weege and other visuals of social unrest; a 12-minute taped narration; articles on the topic; four 12" x 18" posters; and a teacher's study guide.

The Arts and Crafts in Kenyan Society
Includes 82 slides taken in Kenya showing craftsmen and artists at work and the objects they produce; an 18-minute taped narration; articles on the topic; and a teacher's study guide.

The Street as a Creative Vision:
Includes 80 slides of the street as seen by painters and photographers from 1850 through landscape architects of today, tracing the change in societal values as reflected in the street; articles on the topic; one 12" x 18" poster; and a teacher's study guide including a script to be read with the slides. (There is no tape with this package.)

Frank Lloyd Wright: On Behalf of Life:
Includes 80 slides of Frank Lloyd Wright and his work; an interview with Mr. Wright emphasizing art and education; articles on the topic; a poster; and a study guide.

FILMS

The Artist and His Work:
Illustrates the role of the artist in society via the work of three painters, a sculptor, a potter, and a weaver. Begins with exploring the source of their ideas and follows the development of individual pieces. Ends with describing the function of galleries and art centers in disseminating this work to the public. Catalogue #7744
28 min., color, 16mm
Cost: $200.00   Rental fee: $6.75

Developing Creativity:
Shows the need for creativity in dealing with current societal problems. Explores the role of art experiences in developing creative attitudes among students. Uses a high school pottery class as an example. Catalogue #7900
11 min., color, 16mm
Cost: $100.00   Rental fee: $3.50

Both films available from the:
Bureau of Audio-Visual Instruction
University of Wisconsin-Extension
1327 University Avenue
Madison, Wisconsin 53706
Please specify catalogue number when ordering.

OTHER PUBLICATIONS

The Wisconsin Monographs of Visual Arts Education:
Published by the Department of Art, University of Wisconsin-Madison. Each issue is devoted to a topic concerning the visual arts in a broad educational context.

#1   Artists and Art Education
#2   Extra-School Art Education
#3   Museums and Art Education
Cost: $1.00 each.

NEXT ISSUE
Education and the Arts

SUBSCRIPTION INFORMATION

Arts in Society is currently issued three times a year. Subscription will begin with the issue current at time of order unless otherwise specified.

Special professional and student discounts are available for bulk subscription orders. Inquire for information.

For change of address, please send both old and new addresses and allow six weeks to effect change. Claims for missing numbers must be submitted no later than two weeks after receipt of the following issue.

Please **address all subscription correspondence** to:
Administrative Secretary
ARTS IN SOCIETY
University of Wisconsin-Extension
610 Langdon Street
Madison, Wisconsin 53706

Make checks payable to *Arts in Society*. Wisconsin residents: Please add 4% sales tax.

ORDER FORM

Please enter my subscription and/or send me the items indicated:

NAME_____

ADDRESS_____

CITY_____ STATE_____ ZIP_____

Subscription Rates:
☐ 1 year or 3 issues: $7.50
☐ 2 years or 6 issues: $14.00
☐ 3 years or 9 issues: $20.00
☐ 1 year, student subscription: $6.50

Back Issues Still Available:
☐ V6#3 The Arts of Activism $3.50
☐ V7#1 The Sounds and Events of
        Today's Music $3.50
☐ V7#2 The Electric Generation $3.50
☐ V7#3 The California Institute of
        the Arts: Prologue to a
        Community $3.50
☐ V8#1 Search for Identity and
        Purpose $3.50
☐ V8#2 The Arts and the Human
        Environment $3.50
☐ V8#3 The Theatre: Does It Exist? $3.50
☐ V9#1 Environment and Culture $3.50
☐ V9#2 The Communications
        Explosion $3.50
☐ V9#3 The Social Uses of Art $3.50
☐ V10#1 The Humanist Alternative $3.50
☐ V10#2 Film: New Challenge,
        New Possibilities $3.50
☐ V10#3 The Politics of Art $3.50

Instructional Resource Packages:
☐ Art and Technology $50.00
☐ Art and Environment $50.00
☐ Art and Social Revolution $50.00
☐ Arts & Crafts in Kenyan Society $50.00
☐ The Street as a Creative Vision $40.00
☐ Frank Lloyd Wright: On Behalf of Life
    $50.00

Wisconsin Monographs: @$1.00
☐ Artist & Art Education
☐ Extra-School Art Education
☐ Museums & Art Education

Women in the Arts Organizations
Please send me information on:
☐ Wisconsin Women in the Arts
☐ Women in the Arts (national)

Would you spend $5 for a magazine that shows you how to walk on water, raise the dead and make angels of mere mortals?

No miracle is too great for the behind-the-scenes professional.

Yours are the costumes and scenery that set Shaw's *Inferno* ablaze. Whose lighting brings out the best in Olivier. Whose direction keeps the freshman class from falling flat on its face.

And often you manage on what seems little more than a borrowed shoelace and your own creativity.

So to make the task a bit easier, there's THEATRE CRAFTS. The magazine with the professional know-how that helps you turn the impossible into the beautiful.

In each issue you'll discover a host of how-to articles on lighting, set design, make-up, costuming, music, film and so much more!

THEATRE CRAFTS is diagrams and drawings. Candid, no-nonsense dialogues with backstage masters. And the best of the best from their decades of professional experience.

And it's all yours. In the magazine that's all yours.

THEATRE CRAFTS. Especially written for the people who never take a curtain call.

RECENT THEATRE CRAFTS ARTICLES:

The Philosophy of Costuming

Street Theatre

Face Painting and Furnishings

Who Goes to an American Play?

Creative Recycling
Is a Budget Boon

Theatre for Theatre

Managing a Regional Theatre
Costume Shop

Show me how!   ATS-7

Please enter my subscription to THEATRE CRAFTS, 33 E. Minor St., Emmaus. Pa. 18049 for:

☐ 1 year (6 issues) $5.00   ☐ 2 years (12 issues) $9.00

NAME_____

TITLE OR FUNCTION_____

ADDRESS_____

CITY_____STATE_____ZIP_____

THEATRE OR ORGANIZATION_____

☐ PAYMENT ENCLOSED

☐ BILL ME

☐ RENEWAL

☐ *Please send me information on group rate subscriptions.*